The Princess and the Peace Corps

The Princess and the Peace Corps

Lorena Anne Hulskamp

iUniverse, Inc.
New York Lincoln Shanghai

The Princess and the Peace Corps

Copyright © 2006 by Lorena Anne Hulskamp

All rights reserved. No part of this book may be used or reproduced by any means, graphic, electronic, or mechanical, including photocopying, recording, taping or by any information storage retrieval system without the written permission of the publisher except in the case of brief quotations embodied in critical articles and reviews.

iUniverse books may be ordered through booksellers or by contacting:

iUniverse
2021 Pine Lake Road, Suite 100
Lincoln, NE 68512
www.iuniverse.com
1-800-Authors (1-800-288-4677)

The views expressed in this work are solely those of the author and do not necessarily reflect the views of the publisher, and the publisher hereby disclaims any responsibility for them.

ISBN-13: 978-0-595-41869-5 (pbk)
ISBN-13: 978-0-595-86216-0 (ebk)
ISBN-10: 0-595-41869-4 (pbk)
ISBN-10: 0-595-86216-0 (ebk)

Printed in the United States of America

This book is dedicated to

Brenda Sue Drew

Renwick Nelson

Charles Clayton Hayes

These three names are on the list of thousands of Americans who have served as volunteers in the past 45 years of Peace Corps

My name is also on that list.

However, without these three I doubt it would be.

And I know that without their steadfast friendship, support and, most of all, sense of humor, I never would have been inspired to write this book.

Contents

PREFACE. xiii
THE DECISION. 1
THE PREPARATION 6
THE JOURNEY 8
THE COUNTRY. 20
ORIENTATION 22
HOMESTAY 37
SWEARING-IN. 56
RETURN TO NUKU'ALOFA 60
A PERILOUS SITUATION .62
SALVATION 75
PALANGEVILLE. 78
TUPOU HIGH SCHOOL 83
HOME AT LAST. 87
2001: A TONGAN ODYSSEY 96
SEPTEMBER 11, 2001 120
LIFE GOES ON. 125
TWO THOUSAND AND TWO 134
CLOSE OF SERVICE 140

FROM THE DUKE & THE DUCHESS, RENWICK NELSON
   & BRENDA SUE DREW 145

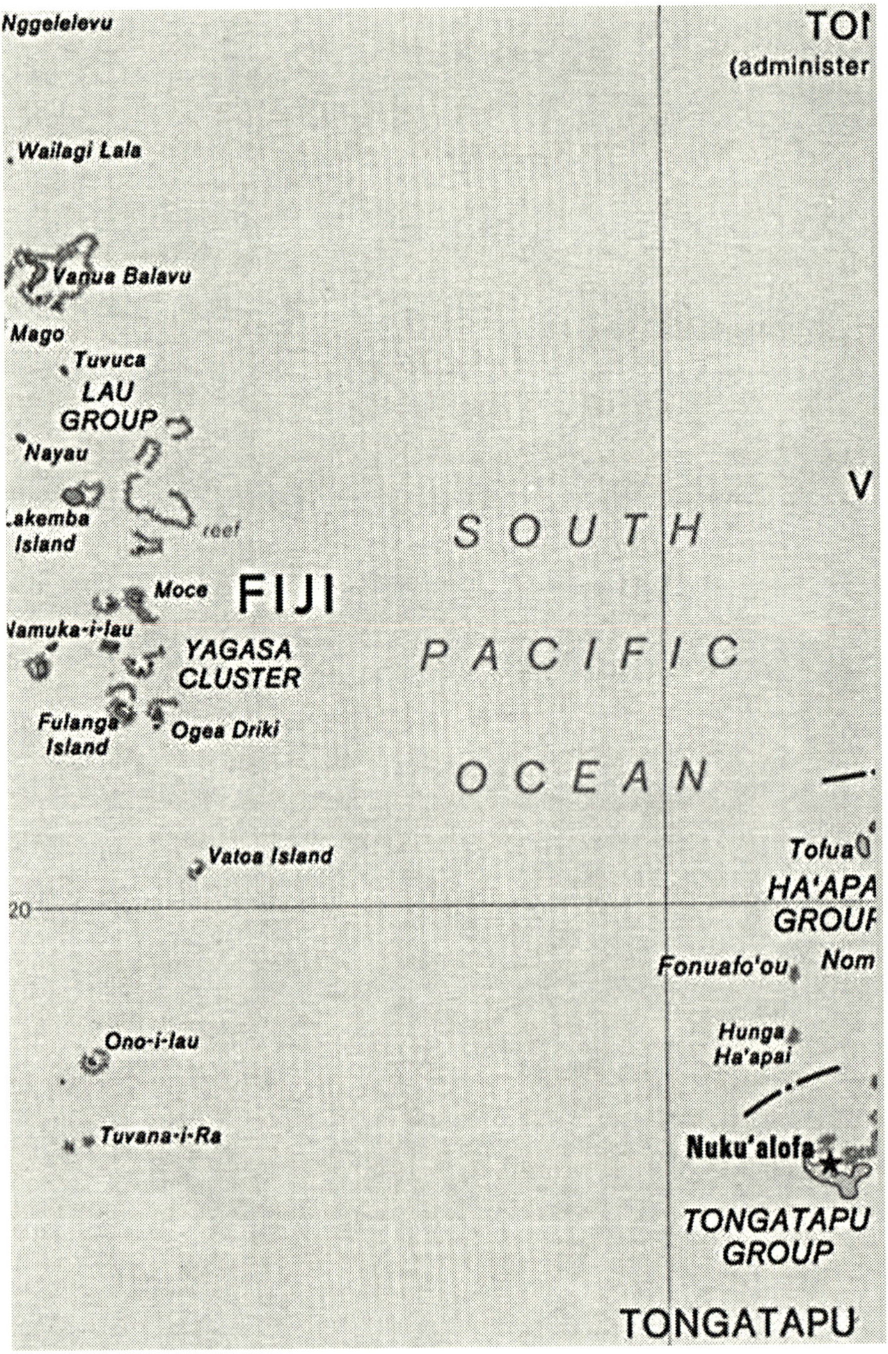
Nggelelevu
TON
(administer
Wailagi Lala
Vanua Balavu
Mago
Tuvuca
LAU
GROUP
Nayau
Lakemba
Island
reef
SOUTH
PACIFIC
OCEAN
V
Moce
FIJI
Namuka-i-lau
YAGASA
CLUSTER
Fulanga
Island
Ogea Driki
Vatoa Island
Tolua
HA'APA
GROUP
20
Fonuafo'ou
Nom
Hunga
Ha'apai
Ono-i-lau
Tuvana-i-Ra
Nuku'alofa
TONGATAPU
GROUP
TONGATAPU

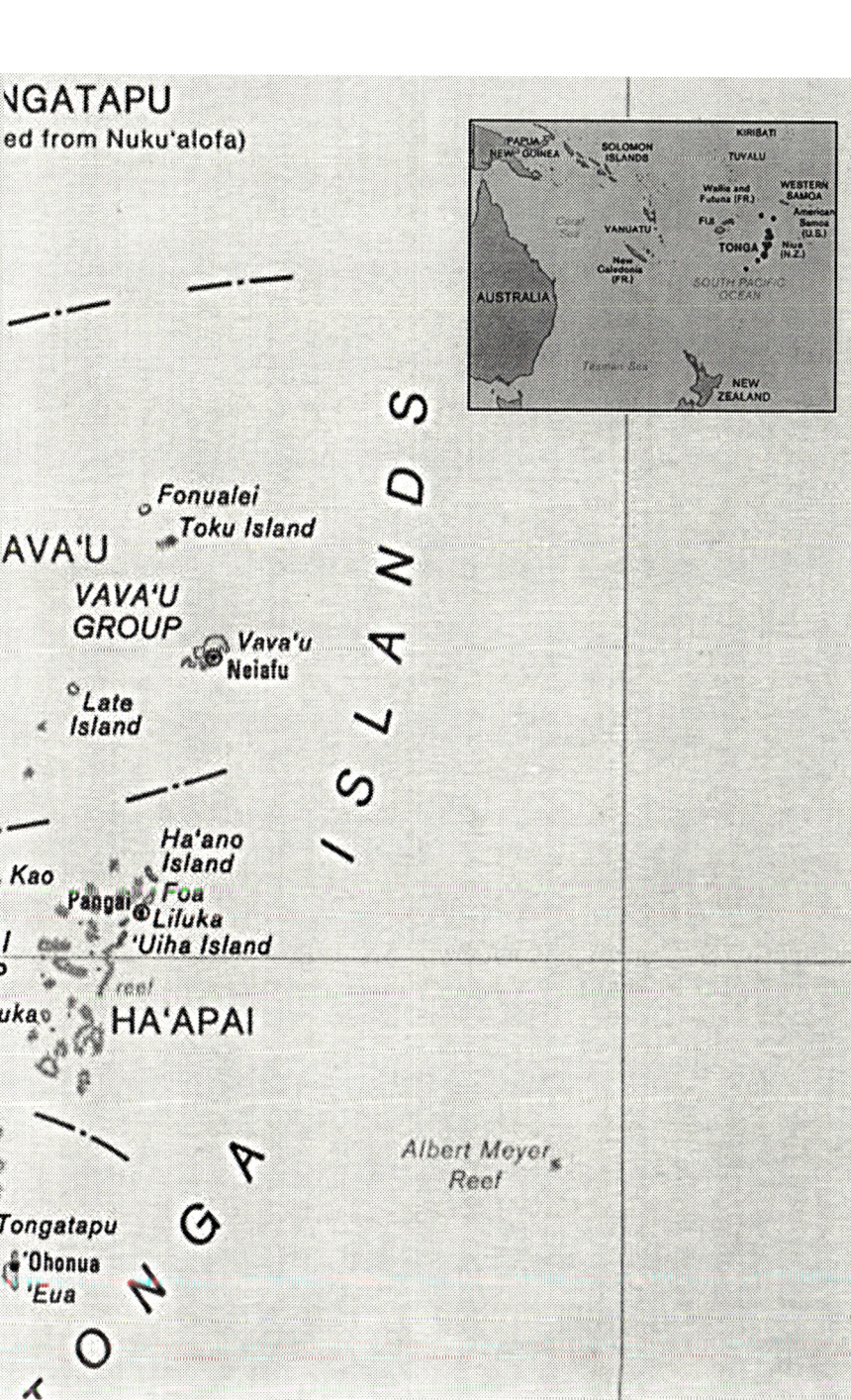

PREFACE

The story you are about to read is of a Peace Corps volunteer's experience.

I have thought a great deal as to whether or not serving in the Peace Corps is a life-changing experience.

The Peace Corps is difficult, to say the least. It is not for everyone: the living conditions are challenging, likewise, accepting and appreciating another culture takes time.

The fast-paced, time-is-money, and look-out-for-number-one American way of life is what we are accustomed to. The technology, the luxuries, and the choices available to us are hard to let go.

In my country of service, for the most part, the people were born, raised, lived and died without ever leaving the island. There was the concept that there is nothing but time. It is as if without ever reading the book, they quote my favorite literary character, "After all, tomorrow is another day."

I believe what happens is that the Peace Corps service takes undeveloped altruistic qualities we all have and brings them to the surface. The experience enhances, strengthens and makes us mindful of the need to discover these dormant facets of ourselves.

If you finish your two-year service, it is true that you will never be the same. During a period of self-doubt in my service, one of my closest friends, Debra Tucker, sent me a quote: "A mind once expanded can never return to its original shape." It was just the gold nugget I needed and one that I will always treasure.

Sometimes you need a lot of rain to really appreciate the sun. Sometimes you must choose whether to laugh or cry.

There are probably as many different reasons for joining the Peace Corps as there are volunteers. And even though the volunteers work together and assist each other in the country of service, both professionally and personally, each one will have a different tale to tell.

This is my story.

Peace: 1. A state of harmony between people or groups. 2. A state of tranquility or serenity.

Corps: 1. A group or persons associated or acting together.

Princess: 1. A non-reigning female member of a royal family. 2. Daughter of a sovereign.

Sovereign: 1. A supreme ruler. 2. Supreme in rank, power or authority. 3. Having independence; autonomous: a sovereign state.

THE DECISION

Once upon a time in America, there was a Princess.

Well, not *actually* a princess, as she was not a member of a Royal Family. As you know, in America we do not have a Royal Family. Still, in America we have many "princesses." These are daughters, usually the only girl, in a family where the father is the Supreme Ruler. He is the undisputed master of all he surveys. He has absolute rank, power and authority of his domain (his family). Thus, he is a Sovereign; therefore, the daughter is a Princess.

I know, I looked it up. The definition of a princess: "daughter of a sovereign" and "non-reigning female member of the family." The mother is the reigning female, a.k.a the Queen, but don't let this fool you. The Princess also wields plenty of power.

The Princess is trained from birth that she is entitled to almost anything she desires.

The King and Queen are not aware of any wrongdoing. They just want their little Princess to be happy.

The Princess in my story was not a stupid little Princess. She learned at a young age to survey the situation and assume the appropriate demeanor to achieve her goals.

Meaning: some occasions called for a sweet smile, accompanied by a soft, pleading voice, while others required a foot stomping, combined with a show of anger, and if extreme measures were demanded, there were always tears. These skills never failed her.

Eventually, our Princess was all grown up. And, I mean really grown up—forty-five years old. She was rather spoiled and very bored. She was searching for something—something to strive for, aspire to; a quest, an adventure.

What she found was the Peace Corps.

The Peace Corps is a branch of the United States government. President Kennedy founded the Peace Corps in 1961. Forty years later, the Peace Corps had seen tremendous growth, with over seven thousand volunteers serving in seventy-two countries worldwide. The Peace Corps volunteers use their varied skills in third world countries, training, educating, and guiding others who have not had the benefits and advantages Americans have had towards improving their lives. The Peace Corps is the only U.S. organization where the volunteers live like and with the locals, observing and respecting the traditions of that country. The organization is billed as "the toughest job you'll ever love."

At first, you might wonder how this would appeal to our Princess. But think about it: living overseas for two years with six weeks vacation to travel to surrounding countries, with full medical provided. After all, what Princess doesn't love to travel? Besides, any Princess worth her tiara should live abroad at some point in her life. In addition, our Princess was well versed at socializing, and she could make small talk and friends easily. She would never go to someone's house empty-handed. On top of these qualifications for the Peace Corps, she knew that this institution comes with built-in companions, like a sorority, a fraternity, or an elite club. She would be uniting with others of her own ilk for a common goal. This sounded like just what the Princess has been looking for. Come on, how "tough" can it be?

So, the Princess sent her application off to the Peace Corps headquarters in Washington, D.C.

Meanwhile, she notified her friends and members of the Royal Family of her decision.

There were some scoffs and some laughter.

A few "You and the Peace Corps? You're kidding, right?"

The Queen mother was adamant: "I absolutely forbid it."

The ex-husband proclaimed, "That would be the best thing that could happen to you, short of a sound thrashing."

The Princess let this negativity wash over her like a cleansing rain.

When one of her previous coworkers said, "Do you remember when the company we worked for closed? For moral support, six of us went to the unemployment office together. *You* showed up in a full-length fur coat, diamond earrings, a Louis Vuitton handbag and three-inch heels! At the *unemployment* office!" To this the Princess had a response: "What's your point?"

When any Princess experiences a period of vexation, she nevertheless must continue to place her best foot, or shoe, forward.

There was a modest group of supporters for her decision. Yet, even from her most ardent advocates came the constant refrain, "What will you *do*?"

In addition to her basic Princess training, the Princess was not without other expertise. She was a buyer for a major department store for many years. She owned and operated her own shop, and was a vice-president of merchandising for a large specialty store chain. It's pretty universal that Princesses excel at retail. What is retail, really? Shopping and spending someone else's money. The Princess applied to the Peace Corps as a small business volunteer.

The application process seemed like a test in tenacity, with all the legal forms, medical evaluations, dental x-rays, blood tests, vision, hearing, etc. Then there were the essays, "Why do you want to do this?" "What do you feel you have to offer?" and "How will you handle the cultural differences?" Well, our Princess was determined. She had resolve. She had stamina. The Princess wrote her essays, filed all the legal documents and was poked and prodded by every branch of the medical profession. Finally she prevailed.

The Peace Corps called for an interview!

When the Princess got this message, she was very excited.

The Princess was instructed to choose a time for a scheduled telephone interview. She was informed that if the applicant lived near a regional office, then personal interviews were conducted. The applicant would not be compensated for any expenditures getting to/or from the interview, consequently, most interviews were conducted by phone. The Princess lived on the ocean in Palm Beach, Florida—the nearest regional office was Atlanta, Georgia.

Our Princess was surrendering two years of her life. She wanted to see an office, meet some employees and make sure this was the right "sort" of commitment for a Princess to make.

The Princess made an appointment with a recruiter in the Atlanta offices of the Peace Corps. Then she purchased a plane ticket and winged her way to her destiny. This might seem a bit immoderate to some, but not to our Princess. Besides, the ex-husband had a house in Atlanta where she could stay. And her only son, the Little Prince, was attending Emory University. All in all, she knew this would make for a pleasant excursion.

On the appointed day, the Little Prince drove the Princess to the Peace Corps offices in downtown Atlanta. If the truth were told, the Little Prince thought his mother was going through a phase. The Little Prince was not entirely "unspoiled" himself. Still, the Little Prince loved the Princess and he did his best to put forth a show of support. He dropped the Princess off in front of a large and imposing building. No cheap digs. The Princess saw this as a good sign. Inside, the Peace Corps office was quite nicely appointed. The people were well groomed and friendly. The Princess was surer and surer of her plan. A young woman introduced herself as the recruiter and ushered the Princess to a conference room. The Princess and the recruiter connected immediately. The Princess asked how she could best contribute. The recruiter mentioned several possibilities; however, the placement officer in Washington would make the final decision. The recruiter's job was to weed out and/or make a recommendation to nominate an applicant. The Princess had one stipulation: "No place cold." So, as the Princess and the recruiter shook hands, the recruiter assured the Princess she would hear from the Peace Corps soon.

Several weeks later, a large packet arrived at the Princess's home. She was offered an assignment in the Kingdom of Tonga, in the South Pacific. The job was described as working with the youth of Tonga, a startup project called the Future Farmers of the Pacific.

Well, our Princess was ecstatic with the location! The South Pacific! Visions of exquisite sandy beaches, swaying palm trees, and exotic birds danced in her head. Polynesians wearing flower leis and sarongs—definitely Princess territory!

However, the word *farmer* was not in the Princess's vocabulary.

Farmer: a person who cultivates land; a grower, raiser, tiller, agriculturist.

To farm: plow, hoe, plant, sow, raise, grow, reap, harvest.

This could be a problem. I know of no Princesses with genuine agriculture experience. The only plants our Princess was familiar with were the long-stemmed varieties delivered in tissue paper with a big red bow and a nice card. They couldn't possibly mean that the Princess herself would have to plow, hoe, plant, sow, raise, grow, reap or harvest. Wouldn't this be rather harsh on her nails?

The Princess placed a telephone call to headquarters. She inquired as to exactly what part of actual "farming" was involved with the Future Farmers? She was informed, "Why, none at all. This is a marketing position." As a matter of fact, the Princess had been specifically chosen for this assignment precisely because of her extensive marketing background.

Ah, yes, yes, our Princess did have over twenty years marketing experience. She was adroit at special events, quite ingenious at sales promotions and, uniquely clever with advertising. She had coordinated, commentated and facilitated many a fabulous fashion show. Nevertheless, she was unclear how her past endeavors related to farming.

"You won't actually be out in the field growing things," the officer in D.C. assured the Princess. "You will advise the youth about stock projections, selling the product, finding overseas buyers. Strictly marketing. *After* they have grown whatever it is."

Her doubts overcome, the Princess accepted the position. She was confident she could market *anything*, even if it was probably dirty

THE PREPARATION

What does a Princess pack for two years? What essentials can a Princess not be without? What necessities are truly indispensable?

She must start with the basics: shampoo, conditioner, mousse, hair spray, soap, shower gel, loofah, face cleansers, toner, moisturizer, dental floss, toothpaste and whitening strips. She mustn't forget the hair dryer, curling iron and electric toothbrush; foundation, blush, eye shadow, eyelash curler, mascara and, of course, lipstick, lots of lipstick. No Princess could ever be caught dead without her lipstick in place. Nail files, nail polish, polish remover, cotton balls, and nail clippers will be needed. Face wipes, Q-tips, Vaseline, bug spray, magnifying mirror, tweezers and scissors cannot be left behind. What about tape, needle and thread, glue, batteries, cassettes and books?

Definitely the Ralph Lauren sheets and the Chanel sunglasses must be included.

Then, of course, there is the requisite Princess trousseau. How many coordinated, ensembles, shoes with matching bags; and which accessories should she take? She must be prepared for all occasions.

As our Princess packed she remembered reading somewhere not to take shorts or tank tops. There was some mention about this being a religious country and the females must keep their shoulders and legs covered at all times. Surely, they couldn't mean no cruise wear at all! It must be very hot over there.

Better safe than sorry, was the Princess's motto. In her youth, she had been a Girl Scout—something the Royal Family rarely spoke of. During the annual cookie drive, the Princess felt that traipsing door-to-door to sell one or two boxes of cookies seemed unproductive. She stood outside the door of the major supermarket and sold her cookies in no time. The Scout Leader informed the Princess that this was not the essence of the cookie drive. The Princess was unceremoniously evicted from the troop. As we all know, nowadays this is common practice amongst the Girl Scouts. As usual, the Princess was ahead of her time.

The planning, sorting, adding and eliminating took weeks. The Queen convinced the Princess not to take the "good" luggage. The Princess discovered a place called the Sports Authority where she purchased three extremely large and one medium-sized duffle bags. She took her eighteen-speed bike to a bicycle shop, where it was revamped and boxed; she also packed twenty-four spare tires, a tool kit and an instruction book. Not that the Princess had any intention of reading the manual herself, but it might come in handy for whoever would assist her with bike repair.

Finally, the Princess had everything packed and she was ready to go.

There was one last thing to do. The Peace Corps advised against bringing jewelry of any kind. The evening before she departed, the Princess left with the Queen her diamond earrings, diamond tennis bracelet and twenty-four-karat gold watch with the Austrian crystal face. She locked away her tanzanite earrings from her safari in Kenya and her cartouche from her cruise down the Nile in Egypt.

She arose early on the appointed day, showered and dressed conservatively, for a Princess, in an outfit specifically chosen for the auspicious occasion. She enjoyed her last morning in Florida, outside on the balcony, overlooking the waves crashing onto the beach, savoring her daily ritual of two Diet Cokes and smokes. She felt secure in the knowledge that she had six cartons of her cigarettes safely tucked away in her three oversized duffels. Our Princess was nobody's fool. She realized that her brand of extra long (120) menthol cigarettes could not be purchased on just any street corner, even in Palm Beach. She had another carton in her carryon, and a solemn oath from the King and Queen that she would receive a shipment of four cartons every month.

Last, she strapped on her only concession to the no-jewelry rule, a brand new plastic digital watch. Hoping the plastic won't give her a rash, the Princess headed to the airport.

Let the adventure begin!

THE JOURNEY

The Princess was to fly to San Francisco and check in to the designated hotel where a staging meeting was scheduled for 1:00 p.m. At this gathering, the group going to Tonga would meet each other. Two representatives of the Peace Corps would prepare them for what was to happen over the next two years.

The problem facing our Princess was her luggage. She would only be at the hotel for one night, returning to the airport in twenty-four hours to fly to Tonga. The Princess had three huge, extra-large duffel bags, one medium-sized duffle bag, her backpack, one carryon and the boxed bike. All of this would be very difficult to transport from the airport to downtown San Francisco then back the next day. Since the Princess had what she needed for one night in her carryon, she simply walked off the plane and into a Super Shuttle, trusting that the airport would hold all of her unclaimed luggage until she returned.

Entering the hotel, she checked in at the reception desk. She was given her room key and notified that her roommate had not yet arrived. Oh! That's fine. The Princess did not realize she would be sharing a room, but that made sense, saves on expenses. Whoever this person would be, she had to jump through the same hoops the Princess did. She had been evaluated and approved. Since the girl was Peace-Corps approved, then she would undoubtedly be Princess approved.

In her room there were two double beds, and her natural impulse was to claim the "better" bed. Implausible as it may seem, our Princess believed in Karma. If she took the more desirable bed, she thought, she might be paid back tenfold for her show of greediness. So she selected the double bed against the wall and left for her unknown roommate the superior one.

Plucking a Diet Coke from the minibar, the Princess relaxed on the balcony with a smoke.

It had been a long time since the Princess had a roommate—not since she was a department store buyer. The first week of every month, all the buyers went to New York City for the buying trips. The girls always shared rooms. One eventful trip, they tripled up, and three of the girls decided to get a two-bedroom suite. The Princess and one of the girls (Buyer K) went early in the morning that Sunday, instead of Sunday night, so they could get in a full day of shopping for themselves. Buyer E was not joining them until that evening.

Dashing to their suite to drop off the luggage, they discovered there was only one bedroom attached to a large living room. They called the front desk to complain. They had reserved TWO bedrooms. They were informed there were none available, but that the single bedroom across the hall was also theirs. Well, they couldn't waste precious shopping time arguing about this. They were there first; when Buyer E arrived she would just have to take the room across the hall.

The Princess and her friend were on a mission. They shopped all afternoon, finishing up the day with cocktails at the comedy club Catch a Rising Star. Here Buyer K had *way* too much to drink. Our Princess was by no means a teetotaler—in fact she was usually the one that imbibed a little too much—but for some reason this evening Buyer K was on a roll. Late in the evening Buyer K turned to the Princess and said, "We have to leave! *Right now*!!" She walked out. The Princess grabbed the waitress, threw some money at her, and followed Buyer K into the street. She found her companion swaying on the curb. The Princess practically threw herself in front of a yellow cab, shoved her friend in the back seat and headed for the hotel.

When they opened the door to their suite, Buyer E was in her nightie on the couch painting her toenails. Buyer K immediately went through the bedroom to the bathroom, closing the door behind her, leaving the Princess to fight it out with Buyer E.

"Hey, we were here first. *You* get the room across the hall."

"No way," Buyer E exclaimed. "I have already unpacked and I am in my pajamas. One of you can go across the hall."

The Princess heard a noise from the bedroom. Investigating, she found Buyer K sprawled out, fully dressed, across the bed. She was unconscious. Then the Princess entered the bathroom where her unfortunate pal had been ill. All over the place! So the Princess wheeled her still unpacked suitcase into the sitting room. She faced Buyer E: "Fine, if you really want to stay in here I will go across the hall."

Buyer E stated, "Yes, I really want to stay here."

So the Princess bid her goodnight and rolled across the hall into the bedroom with the nice clean bathroom.

Enough reverie; it was almost one o'clock. The Princess went to the conference room indicated. The two Peace Corps employees were there, but she was the first of her group to arrive. She was told that the group was small, only six of them, counting her. Waiting for the others, the Princess anticipated she would be the oldest. She was pleasantly surprised when a couple in their early fifties were the next to come in. The three chatted. They were both well dressed and quite attractive and they were also from Florida. The two were from Jacksonville, just a few hours up the coast from the Princess. Upon further discussion they discovered that they had the same recruiter in Atlanta. The wife had brought her laptop computer and a digital camera and she had already created a Web site to share their exploits with others. They were ready for a big adventure. Well, any Princess realizes instantly when she is in the presence of other Royals. And so, this was how our Princess first encountered the two who would later become her closest friends, confidants and eventual neighbors over the next two years: the Duke and the Duchess.

Three here, three to go. A young man was the next to enter. Twenty something, a little disheveled and with the wildest mane of long, corkscrew curls the Princess has seen since Shirley Temple. The Dude.

Next came the much-anticipated roommate. She was also twenty something, bubbly, perky (all princesses hate perky) and for no apparent reason, this young lady seemed to hold a very high opinion of herself. The Princess was not sure what to make of her, yet.

Lastly, an extremely tall guy joined them, six feet five inches, and he appeared to be in his late thirties. He was quiet and unpretentious, to be known as the Quiet One. "Well, well, the gang's all here," the Princess thought.

The agenda of the meeting was several "get to know you" exercises, discussions of their feelings and expectations and a timetable of events for the next few days.

The group was to depart San Francisco the next afternoon on a thirteen-hour overnight flight to Auckland, New Zealand. In Auckland, after a twelve-hour layover, they would continue on to Tonga. They would arrive approximately 10:30 p.m. on Saturday night, Tongan time, Tonga being fourteen hours ahead of our West Coast.

The Peace Corps representatives needed one of the six to be responsible for the group—to keep track of the luggage, make sure no one was lost along the way and deliver to Peace Corps Tonga their medical records.

The Quiet One had been in the Peace Corps right after college. He had served two tours, back-to-back in Togo and The Gambia, Africa. Even though this was a number of years ago, he was chosen for this duty because of his prior experience.

When the meeting adjourned, everyone went to his or her room. This put the Princess and her roommate alone. The young girl announced she was going out with a group of friends, and she expected a particular young man to join her. The young girl asked if the Princess would mind if she brought her young man back to spend the night with her.

The Princess was astounded. "In *this* room? Right there, in the bed next to *me*?" The Princess was an adult. She was no prude. She was not a puritan, but this was too much. "It's one thing to share a room with a complete stranger the Peace Corps has approved," she thought. "It's quite another for that stranger to bring another stranger of the opposite sex into the room!"

Yes, the Princess did mind! Quite a lot, actually! How ill bred, how uncouth, how *common*!

The next morning, when the Princess awoke, she was pleased to discover that the Commoner was alone in her bed. However, she was not pleased to discover, on second glance, that the girl was completely naked!

The Princess hurriedly showered and dressed. She was anxious to let the Commoner have the room all to herself. In the lobby she happened upon the Duke and the Duchess. They asked what did the Princess do the night before that she could not join the group for dinner. The Princess had no idea what they were talking about. Soon it became clear that the Commoner had approached each of them individually and invited everyone in the group to accompany her and her friends for dinner. Everyone, that is, *except* the Princess. In addition, when the others asked where the Princess was, the Commoner told them, "She said she had other plans," implying the Princess felt she was too good for them. The Princess was aghast! It was obvious she was intentionally *not* invited. How could that be? The Princess was accustomed to being the first on the guest list! The Princess was fuming—why, that little whippersnapper! Immediately, her regal training kicked in. She smiled, apologized, "Sounds like everyone had a great time. I am so sorry I couldn't join you. Do include me next time. I wouldn't miss it for the world."

In the lobby a sign had been posted: "Peace Corps Volunteers: Free time this morning. The bus to the airport will depart the hotel at 1:00 p.m. Everyone meet in the lobby with your bags at 12:30 p.m."

They were all there at 12:30 sharp. The Peace Corps representatives were giving parting instructions to the Quiet One as group leader. The Princess observed the Quiet One being handed a wad of yellow strings of yarn. The Quiet One turned first to the Duke and the Duchess and said, "These yellow strings are to easily identify all of our luggage. You need to tie one to each of your bags except your backpack. How many do you need?" The Duke and the Duchess needed two.

When the Quiet One walked over to talk to the Dude, the Princess leaned close to the Duchess. "What about the rest of your things?"

The Duchess replied, "What do you mean the rest?" The Duke and the Duchess had one suitcase and a backpack each. The Duchess had her laptop and digital camera in another shoulder bag.

The Princess glanced around. The Dude was attaching his one piece of yarn to his bag. The Commoner had accepted one string. Oh no, the Princess was the only person with more than one bag, way more!

The Quiet One approached her. "How many strings do you need?"

Princess: "I have a boxed bike, does that count?"

The Quiet One: "Yep, it goes on everything but your backpack."

Princess: "Well…then…I guess I need six."

The Quiet One gave the Princess a quick double take. "How many?"

Now our Princess was embarrassed. "Six," she repeated.

The Quiet One questioned, "Six?"

Now the Princess was not only embarrassed but also irritated. She snapped at him, "Yes, six. It comes after five and before seven."

Smiling, the Quiet One handed her the yarn. "Okay, six it is."

He turned away and announced to the group, "Is everybody ready? Let's get on the bus."

Great, the Princess thought, it's the first full day, and I have already been humiliated and embarrassed! What next?

While she was ascending the steps of the bus, the Princess heard the Commoner say to the Dude, "Six, she brought *six* bags!"

The Dude replied, "Cool, I know where to borrow anything I forgot."

As the Princess settled in her seat for the ride to the airport, she thought to herself that she would not have a problem with the Dude, the Duke or the Duchess. She would need to keep an eye on that Commoner and the jury was still out on the Quiet One.

At the airport, the Princess had to go back to the domestic terminal and claim all of her luggage. She engaged a skycap to transport everything to the international terminal. There she was promptly charged $125.00 excess baggage fees.

The overnight flight to Auckland was interminable, but uneventful. The Princess and the Duchess discussed their mutual zest for sunbathing, pedicures and massages. They exchanged ideas on how to decorate, modestly of course; their anticipated Peace Corps abodes. They marveled at how lucky they were to have gotten the South Pacific. Surely, they had won the Peace Corps Sweepstakes, an island paradise!

A few rows up the aisle, the Dude and the Quiet One sat together. The Commoner chose the row behind them. She spent most of the night flight standing up leaning over their seatbacks, chatting them up. Obviously, the Duke, Duchess and Princess were of little interest and no use to her.

They crossed the international dateline and lost a day. They departed the United States on a Thursday evening. They arrived in New Zealand on Saturday morning.

The Auckland airport was very nice. There were many upscale shops, duty free stores, banks, restaurants, bars, and Internet access, even day rooms. Unfortunately, the day rooms were all full. Everyone in the group did "hire" a towel and enjoyed a refreshing hot shower. To "hire" in New Zealand translates to "rent."

The really great thing about the Auckland airport was there were smoking lounges! Exactly half the group smoked; only another smoker can appreciate the first cigarette after a thirteen-hour flight. The taste, the flavor, and the aroma—this is truly something to be cherished and shared with others who have the same bad habit. The Princess, the Dude and the Quiet One charged pell-mell into the first small vestibule they found, easily identified from afar by the surrounding mist. They inhaled deeply the visible vapors and poisonous gases given off by the burning cigarettes. Ah, just a little bit of heaven on Earth.

After the smoking, showering and money changing, there was still a good ten hours before the final journey to Tonga. Unanimously, they decided to travel into Auckland. Though it was July in the States, in New Zealand, on the other side of the world, it was the dead of winter. The new recruits were severely underdressed. They unwisely chose a ferry ride over to the resort town of Davenport. The crossing was brutally cold and upon arrival in the small locale, they discovered almost everything was closed for the winter. They did find a quaint café with a large flagstone fireplace boasting a roaring fire. After a leisurely lunch they suffered through the return trip.

Finally it was departure time, with only three more hours to Tonga. No one had slept more than a few hours since Thursday morning. By the time they arrived at their final destination, the Princess had been awake for almost thirty-nine hours. She was spent. She was drained. She was slaphappy. And so was the Duchess; together they giggled, snickered and burst out laughing at absolutely nothing. The plane touched down on the only runway in the capital city, Nuku'alofa. Through the tiny window they could see at least a hundred people waving from the observation deck.

The Duchess said to the Princess, "I think we are in trouble."

"Why?" the Princess asked.

"What if the only thing to do on Saturday night is go to the airport to watch one plane land?"

Tears streamed down their faces as the Duchess and the Princess descended the staircase to their new home for the next two years.

On the other side of customs, the country director and a Peace Corps Tonga staff member greeted them. The Tongan was a giant bear of a man. He was over six feet tall, weighing at least three hundred pounds, and he had close-cropped black hair with a well-trimmed goatee. The country director, an American, came up to about his chest. They were both wearing wrap-around skirts, with what appeared to be straw floor mats tied around their waists. The new arrivals were greeted warmly. The Tongan accounted for all their gear. If he had any reaction to the amount of accouterments the Princess had brought, he gave no indication of it. The Princess immediately decided she liked him.

Outside of the airport were two buses and about forty Peace Corps volunteers, all of them shouting words of welcome and placing flower leis on the new group. As they piled on the buses for the ride to the Peace Corps office, the Duchess whispered to the Princess, "See, this *is* the only thing to do on Saturday night!"

It was nearly midnight as the entourage approached headquarters. Suspended from the second floor, a huge white wooden sign bearing the Peace Corps symbol shone through the inky blackness. The left side of the compound was a two-story edifice. The first floor contained a reception area, an office for the country director, the mailroom, cashier's cage and several other administrative offices. The second floor consisted of three large conference areas, a reference and research library, and numerous additional offices. A drive-through archway connected this structure with the medical building. Behind medical was a small kitchen (known as the tearoom) used by the Tongan staff for work-related cooking. The volunteer's lounge was located next to the tearoom. This area was divided into three rooms. The first large room had the volunteer's mailboxes, one computer for e-mailing, a kitchen and several couches for viewing a TV and VCR. A second room was for storing volunteer's personal belonging during home stays. The third room held three beds, for volunteers overnighting from the outer islands.

Even though it was quite late, the Peace Corps provided a sizable welcome feast. The Princess later discovered this was why so many volunteers came to greet them—free food! The Princess was too exhausted to eat anything. She did desperately want either a Diet Coke or a glass of chilled white wine. Neither was available. In fact, the only beverage she saw was in a large, multicolored round cooler with a tap at the bottom. The only cups were reusable plastic ones, which appeared to have been reused for quite some time. In her mind, the Princess could hear the Queen's voice, "God only knows where those have been." Well, that was all there was, and those were going fast. The Princess quickly grabbed one of the few remaining containers and out through the tap flowed an orange liquid.

She joined a number of volunteers standing off to the side smoking. Lighting one of her extra-long 120 menthol cigarettes, she tasted her drink. *Ew*! This was awful! What was it? After a number of sips she was able to identify what she thought it was: really, really, really watered-down Tang. Our Princess was parched. Well, she thought, if Tang is good enough for the astronauts then it's good enough for me. This is better than nothing. Our Princess didn't know it, but she was already learning. She had three glasses.

It was after 1:00 a.m. when the party concluded. At last, the new arrivals were taken to a guesthouse, and given a fair warning that Peace Corps would be picking them up promptly at 9:30 a.m. for church. Everyone had his or her own room.

This was a fairly large guesthouse and there were other guests staying there as well, and of course at this time of night they were all asleep. The rooms on the first floor were all situated around the outside of a rectangle. In the center was the common area, where people could gather to chat. This was where the sink was, which was not enclosed. This was where there were two toilets and one shower. They were enclosed.

There was a second floor. Upstairs were two bedrooms, a shared toilet and shower and a small sitting area that included an equally small kitchen. The Dude, the Duke and the Duchess had the second floor compartments. The Princess, the Quiet One and the Commoner were on the first floor, along with a number of other guests.

By now, the Princess no longer could count the number of hours since she had slept. Like any other Princess, no matter how exhausted she was, certain duties still had to be performed. She washed her face and she brushed her teeth at the only sink—the only sink being the one in the common area, for all to observe someone performing their private nightly ritual. At this point she was too tired to care, though she realized this would not always be the case. Then the Princess retired to her cubicle, and selected and prepared her outfit for the next day.

There was only one thing left to do before she could slip in between those stiff cotton sheets and rest her royal head on the small, hard sandbag referred to as a pillow. There was one thing that would bring any Princess to her knees. One thing that is, to a Princess, what kryptonite is to Superman. The spider! Finally, after every inch of the room and every possible hiding spot had been scrutinized, our Princess turned off the light. It was 2:50 a.m.

The Princess instantly sank into a deep, dreamless sleep. Suddenly, there was a horrible shrieking noise! The Princess sat straight up in her bed! What was that? My God! There it was again! Surely someone is being attacked, she thought. It seems to be originating right outside the bedroom window!

The Princess leapt out of bed. She turned on her lamp, and then ran to open her door. She peered into the common area, expecting to see lights snapping on all over the guesthouse and alarm bells ringing! There was nothing. What's wrong with everyone? No one could sleep through that!

The noise continued; in fact, it had grown worse! Instead of just one person shrieking, there were many! Still there was no response throughout the guesthouse! Wait, she thought, I know that sound. Somewhere in the recesses of her mind she had heard it before. Not actually in person. Where had she heard it? Where? Wait again. She knew what the sound was. It was from television!

Is it *The Real McCoy's*? Is it *Green Acres*? Why, no, it is a rooster!

Actually, it sounded like a hundred roosters. Yes, that was what that shrieking was. That was why no one was reacting—it was just a hundred roosters crowing at the same time.

But why are there roosters at the guesthouse? she wondered. Why are they crowing? Don't roosters crow at dawn?

The Princess crawled back into her bed. She noticed the time: after four in the morning. It was definitely *not* dawn.

Orientation: 1. To familiarize with new surroundings and circumstances.

Culture: 1. Way of living built upon by a group and transmitted to succeeding generations. 2. A particular form or stage of civilization.

Shock: 1. A sudden disturbance of emotions or sensibilities. 2. To affect with intense surprise, horror or outrage.

Culture shock: 1. Bewilderment and distress experienced by one exposed to a new culture.

Kingdom: 1. A state having a king or queen as its head. 2. An independent realm.

THE COUNTRY

The Kingdom of Tonga is located in Western Polynesia; its nearest neighbor to the west is Fiji and to the north is Samoa.

Tonga consists of 171 islands, spreading over 700,000 square kilometers. The country's population is approximately 100,000 and about two thirds of them live on the main island, Tongatapu.

Tonga's forty-five inhabited islands form four groups. The capital city of Nuku'alofa is on the largest island, Tongatapu. This is where the Peace Corps headquarters are located, and half of the eighty volunteers are placed here. The archipelago of Vava'u is the next largest island group, with a satellite Peace Corps office and approximately twenty volunteers. The volcanic and coral islands of the Ha'apai group rank third with fewer than ten Peace Corps volunteers and no office site. The furthest islands north are the remote volcanic Niuas, Niuafo'ou and Niuatoputapu. These tiny islands are home for only three hundred Tongans and three to five Peace Corps volunteers, with no electricity or running water.

The economy is primarily based on agriculture. The currency is the Pa'anga: US$1 = Tonga $1.98. The official language is Tongan, with English being widely spoken.

The climate is pleasant and slightly cooler than most tropical areas, averaging about 84° F in the summer months, from November to April; winter, May through October, ranges in the high 60s to low 70s.

Tonga is one of the world's few remaining constitutional monarchies. It is the only South Pacific country never to have been colonized by a foreign power. Tonga is ruled by His Majesty King Taufa'ahau Tupou IV.

In every Peace Corps country, there are two Americans administrators, with the balance of the staff consisting of host country nationals. In Tonga, those involved in training are as follows:

- The Peace Corps Country Director (American)
- Assistant Peace Corps Director—Education (American)
- Assistant Peace Corps Director—Youth Work (Tongan)
- Peace Corps Medical Officer (Tongan)
- Training Coordinator (Tongan)
- Lead Trainer (Tongan)
- Two language teachers (Tongan)
- Driver (Tongan)

Each new Peace Corp group is identified by a number. The Princess and her fellow new recruits were known as Group 59. Their eight weeks of training was broken down as follows:

- One week in Tongatapu
- Six weeks home stay in Vava'u, including daily training and language sessions
- Swearing in on September 12, 2000
- Final week in Tongatapu
- Move to individual Peace Corps sites

ORIENTATION

The first full day in Tonga, the volunteers were picked up at 9:30 a.m. and taken to the Kings Church for service.

They had been instructed on the appropriate dress. For the males, this meant long pants and collared shirts. For the females, ankle length skirts were required; also they were to keep their shoulders covered and, of course, nothing low cut was allowed.

This was their first daylight glimpse of Tonga on the five-minute drive to the church. There were small paved roads, few street signs and a surprising number of vehicles for such a tiny island. Wild dogs, pigs and chickens roamed everywhere. The roads were lined with litter. Many Tongans were walking to the church.

Their arrival at the church caused a lot of interest. The locals all knew each other; indeed most were related in some way. The group of white folks stood out in the crowd, providing a little excitement and something to gossip about.

The church was quite large and open, with many rows of wooden pews. At the front was an altar; on the left side were a throne and several other seats separated by a low banister. Obviously, this section was for the king and his entourage. On the right of the altar were two rows of three pews each. This area was for honored guests. This is where the new recruits were seated, all the better to be seen, and to see.

From this vantage point the volunteers got their first good look at the Polynesians. The congregation was large—not just in volume, but also the physical size of the people. The skin color varied from very dark to very light. Everyone had coal-black hair. The women all had long, beautiful hair that they wore in a variety of ways. The younger girls mostly had braids, which looked thick enough to dock a boat. The males were all wearing wrap-around skirts with straw mats around their waists, even the very young male toddlers. The females were dressed modestly, with long skirts and covered shoulders. Some of the ladies had palm frond fans with which to cool themselves. They too, had straw mats or smaller more delicate straw creations tied around their waists.

With much fanfare, the king did arrive. The new recruits had an excellent view of His Majesty, King Taufa'ahau Tupou the IV. Eighty-three years old, he was a large regal-looking man, dressed in an impressive uniform decorated with many metals. He was quite heavy and walked with two canes. He was accompanied by quite a few people. They all sat in the designated throne area. What a thrill for the volunteers to see the king on their first day!

Soon the service began. It started with beautiful singing, a cappella, by the congregation. This was truly lovely. Known for their excellent singing, the Tongans sang in their native tongue, and the beauty transcended all language barriers. Though the church had no funds for an extravagance such as an organ, instruments were not really needed here.

Stragglers kept coming in during the hymns and soon the church filled up. The heat became more oppressive. The sermon was also in Tongan. Even so, the Princess got the message that this was a good old-fashioned fire and brimstone preacher, with his flailing arms and his voice rising and falling in that unmistakable religious cadence. His performance was admirable, but he could not compete with the heat. About three-quarters of the way through the ceremony, the Princess noticed the king was asleep. Of course, he was in a nice cushy throne. The rest of the people were sitting on hard wooden benches that were getting harder by the minute.

Finally, an hour and a half later, the service was over. At last, they were released to the slight stir of air outside. A motorcade of police and fancy cars whisked the king away.

It had been arranged for the volunteers to have a get-together with the training staff for the traditional *umu*.

"Whatever that is," wondered the Princess and the Duchess.

First, they all made a stop back at the guesthouse for the men to change into shorts and t-shirts, while the women were required to remain properly attired. Like the Titanic, the girls were unaware that this was just the tip of the women's rights iceberg.

In each Peace Corps country there is the country director (CD) and usually two assistant Peace Corps directors (APCDs). The volunteers are divided between the two, based on their job assignment.

Drew Havea, a host country national, was one of the APCDs. He was hosting the luncheon. Also present were the CD, the lead trainer, two language teachers, as well as Mrs. Havea and a number of their ten children. The men stayed in the main room, sitting cross-legged on straw mats on the floor, and conversed.

The women were in the kitchen preparing the food. Since few Tongans have an oven, they umu in the yard. To umu, they dig a pit and start a fire. They place coral rocks on top of the fire, layer palm fronds under and over whatever is being cooked and cover it with a mound of dirt. Anything that cannot be umu'ed is cooked on cast iron burners connected to a propane tank.

There were massive quantities of food, most of which the Princess could not identify. There were no paper products of any kind. Later, the Princess discovered these items are quite costly. Cutlery was provided for the volunteers. Tongans use their hands. The guests (the volunteers) went first through the buffet line, then the men and then the women. This was the opposite of America.

The Princess and the Duchess had noticed certain other differences. The Tongan girls were more natural—they did not shave their legs and seemed to be unaware of any unwanted facial hair. The women obviously catered to the men—they waited on them hand and foot. Then, after the men had had their fill, the women did the cleaning also. The Tongans filled their plates several times. The culture reflects an attitude that eating is a great social event to be enjoyed by all at every meal. There are no thoughts of whether the food is healthy or fattening. They are blissfully unaware that Tonga is number one worldwide in obesity and heart disease. Fifteen percent of the population has adult onset diabetes, caused by their diet.

The staff and the new recruits discussed the training schedule. The Princess, the Dude, the Commoner and the Quiet One were all part of the initial start-up project, The Future Farmers of the Pacific. Other volunteers in nearby countries were being trained at the same time for this program. These four would not be notified which island they would be located on till the end of training. This week they would stay at the guesthouse, coming to the PC office each day from 9:00 a.m. to 5:00 p.m. They would have several hours of language instruction each day, along with a variety of other subjects.

The Duke and the Duchess were brought to be teachers; they already knew they would be located on the main island of Tongatapu working at Tupou High in downtown Nuku'alofa. They were replacing a couple that backed out; this is why they were in with the Future Farmers recruits.

The group was introduced to their first Tongan words: *hello* is *malo e lie lie*; *how are you* is *fefe hake*; *thank you* is *malo*; *come* is *h'au*; *go* is *alu*, etc.

They were educated on traditional Tongan clothing. Men do not wear shorts or pants; the customary clothing is the wrap-around skirt called the *tupano* and the *talvala* is the straw mats secured on top of the skirt. There are many varieties of the talvala, from casual for daily wear to very formal ones for important meetings and funerals. The women do not wear anything but dresses or skirts; they too wear talvalas or what is known as a *kia-kia*. This accessory is fashioned like a belt around the waist with long woven strips, of infinite designs, suspended from it.

About 3:30 they were taken back to the guesthouse. Finally the girls got to put on long pants, not truly acceptable attire for any Tongans, though the younger girls were starting to be seen around town, on Saturdays only, in long pants. The times they are a changing, albeit slowly.

They met another volunteer, the Veteran, at the guesthouse. He was in his late 50s and was in from an outer island for medical reasons. This was his fifth time serving as a PCV. He took the Duke, Duchess and Princess for a long walk to show them around.

Since it was Sunday, nothing was open, including the airport and the one television station. The Veteran answered the questions the Princess and the Duchess fired at him. "Where are the beautiful sandy beaches?" "Where are the tropical birds?" "Why is there litter and trash everywhere?"

He explained that there was no beach like the girls were expecting. The shoreline was quite rocky. A person could take a small boat out to a tiny island called Pongi Motu for ten pa'naga, where there was a sandy beach and a wooden snack shop and bar. The boat traveled to and from the island several times a day, of course with the exception of Sunday. There were no tropical birds here; in fact, there were few birds at all, rarely even a seagull.

He explained that there was no garbage pickup. All trash that can be was burned by each family in their backyard. There were at one time big trashcans downtown, but they had to be removed because people were using them. With no one to empty the cans they overflowed, which attracted the wild dogs. The Tongans just tossed any wrapper or soda can as they walked along. It would be too expensive to ship the recyclables to another country, and they threw old cars, appliances, etc., into the ocean where there is a deep trench.

The girls were horrified. What does this do the environment? Don't they worry about the future?

The Veteran explained, "This is the way things have always been. They don't know any different. America did the same thing years ago. People threw everything out the car windows and the like."

Yes, the Princess did remember the Indian Chief with tears in his eyes for the Clean Up America campaign. Still, this was not the island paradise she pictured.

The Princess inquired about the roosters crowing the night before. "I thought roosters only crowed at dawn," she said.

The Veteran educated her. "Usually, there is only one rooster for many hens. Here in Tonga all the hens and roosters roam freely. There is no one to cull the roosters. They crow to stake out their territory and another rooster will crow back, announcing he is there also, and another rooster answers that call, and so on and so on. You'll get used to it. Pretty soon you won't even notice it." The Princess had serious doubts about that.

At four o'clock, the few bakeries on the island opened. A law was passed years ago allowing this, something about a hurricane that had done so much damage to the food crops that people didn't have enough to eat. So the bread shops were granted permission to be open. Though they are called bakeries and they sell all types of bread, they do not sell pastries, pies or cakes. They do have bottled water and Coke light. The four volunteers purchased both of these items. The Tongans say you can drink the tap water, but the Veteran advised against it, claiming the tap water would give you the runs and it tasted bad.

They had eaten such a large late lunch that they didn't need dinner. They all sat and talked in the common area till about 9:00 p.m., then went to bed. Once again the Princess was exhausted. She was asleep almost the minute she closed her eyes, only to be awakened by the "erk, erk, erk, eeeerrrrkkkk" of the roosters at 4:00 a.m. There is no way I will ever be able to sleep through that, she thought.

That Monday they were picked up and taken to the PC office for the official training to begin. Every day started with a prayer—a long, long prayer in Tongan. Every day they had language training. The Princess had no previous language experience except for a few French classes. Tongan words are so long that learning them was difficult. "Malo e lei-lei"—all that just to say hi! She was determined to learn at least the basics of this language. She suggested to the Duke and the Duchess that they practice at night. The Duke informed her that he was too old to learn. Besides, why knock yourself out for a language only 100,000 people in the entire world speak.

They had classes in cross-cultural, medical, and safety issues, like the packs of wild dogs that roam the island, and the molokowo. The Tongans did not have a word in their language for pet. They could not afford pets, as we know them in the States. Any dogs owned were for security reasons only. Stray dogs have reproduced and scavenge for food, then for no apparent reason, they would attack people. No one did anything about this. The Tongans just saw the dogs as part of life. Fortunately, rabies had never been introduced to the island. The molokow is a centipede that at maturity reaches six to eight inches long, with a set of pinchers at one end that inject poison when it stings. The Princess and the Duchess were aghast! Spiders were terrifying enough; now they had a whole new fear!

Each PC country has a Peace Corps Medical Officer (PCMO) just for the volunteers. In Tonga, her office hours were from 8:30 a.m. to 5:00 p.m., Monday through Friday, and she was on call twenty-four hours a day. She informed the volunteers the most common complaint was dog bites or molokow stings.

The training days ended about 5:00 p.m. All the main stores closed at 6:00, so if they needed anything, they needed to get it quick.

The PC office was one block down and two blocks over from "downtown." Downtown you would find the *marketi*, a very large two-story building. The first floor was row after row of tables, where the Tongans bring in their produce to sell. You could never be sure what you would find: potatoes, taro, breadfruit, onions, tomatoes, green peppers or maybe some lettuce. This depended on the season and what crops have fared well. Once in a while, you could find pineapples, oranges, lemons and sweet corn. The second floor of this building was a flea market with booths of clothing, shoes, and odds and ends.

Across the street from the marketi was the main grocery store, Molisi's. This was not to be confused with a Safeway or a Publix. It did have a little bit of everything. The Princess learned the hard way—just because an item is in stock one week doesn't mean it will be in stock the next week, or, for that matter, ever again.

Around the corner was a shop everyone called the Indian Store, because two Fijian men owned and operated it. This was the closest thing to a department store in Tonga, but in the Princess's opinion they would be using that term very loosely.

There were three banks. The Bank of Tonga was where the volunteers opened an account. Here their living allowance was deposited on the 29th of every month, all $180 of it. The second bank was ANZ, the bank of New Zealand. Last was the Tonga Development Bank. There were a number of small shops located around these landmarks. There you have it: downtown Nuku'alofa.

At the end of that first Monday, the traditional kava ceremony was held for the group. Kava is a root that is pounded into a powder, and then mixed with water and stirred with a bunch of straw in a special wooden kava bowl. It is not alcoholic, but it does have the effect of numbing your lips and mouth. In fact, if you drink enough, the next day your whole body will feel numb. Kava is found all over the South Pacific. Each country has a different variety of kava, all claiming theirs to be the most potent.

All volunteers on the island were invited to the country director's house, where a large tent was installed in the yard and many straw mats placed underneath for sitting. The CD sat at one end. At the other end were the women preparing the kava. Preparing the kava involves more than just mixing. It requires special hand movements and specific head motions. In between the two ends, on either side of the mats, were the volunteers. The boys were to sit cross-legged and the girls with their legs tucked sideways under their skirts. Within minutes, the Princess's legs were asleep, and she began to wonder how long all this was going to take.

A respected Tongan elder initiated the ceremony by clapping his hands twice. A young Tongan girl walked in front of him and bowed. The elder called the name of the most important person present, in this case the CD, and clapped again. The CD clapped his hands; the girl retrieved a half of a coconut shell (the drinking vessel) filled with the beverage from the lady who made it. She walked to the CD, bowed, and handed him the drink. He downed it all at once, handed the bowl back to the girl and clapped. The girl returned the coconut shell to be refilled for the next person. This procedure was repeated until everyone had a cup of the brew.

This is the most formal version of the kava ceremony. The tradition is centuries old, and it is considered a great honor to be included in this ritual. Our Princess was very apprehensive. Every single person was drinking out of the same coconut shell; in addition, the mixture had the appearance of a mud puddle, and she did not particularly want her mouth, lips or body numbed. Uh-oh, she thought when her name was called…. She paused…she clapped…she held her breath…swallowed…she clapped…. Thankfully, the rite continued, moving on to another victim. The Princess's lips were numb and the taste was bad, but she has survived.

The guesthouse had no amenities, like little bottles of toiletries. They did supply toilet paper, one roll at a time. The Princess learned that it is advisable to check the status of this commodity before sitting down.

In the common area, people would gather nightly, chatting, smoking, or having a drink. At bedtime, each guest would bring their personals out to the sink to wash up, brush their teeth, etc. Sometimes waiting was required, especially in the morning, for the showers. The Princess discovered that the early riser gets the hot water.

The next day, the group was not picked up by the PC van. Apparently the honeymoon was over. Instead, they walked the twenty minutes to the PC office past the garbage and past the swamp with the pigs wallowing in it. As they walked through the neighborhoods, the poverty was quite apparent. The houses were unpainted or the paint so badly peeling that the original color was questionable. The small children running barefoot were dressed in hand-me-downs. The heat was bearable because this was August, but the Americans could not help but wonder what the summer would be like. The only buildings that were air-conditioned were the Bank of New Zealand and the PC main office (and not the volunteer lounge). They were advised when they got their settling-in allowance that the first thing to buy would be an electric fan. The classes continued each day, the prayer, the language and the cross-cultural. The small group became more like family to each other.

Tuesday night the Princess and the Duchess decided to make use of the small kitchen on the second floor to prepare dinner for the little group. Together, they went to Molisi's, where they selected cheese and a box of macaroni. As neither of the girls knew how to cook, even this simple dish exceeded their talents—the macaroni was too hard and the cheese melted and stuck to the pan. They did have fresh bread, but alas, no oven to toast it in. The guys gave the girls a rough time, however it was apparent they would eat just about anything, especially if they didn't have to pay for it. They finished off the meal with wine and beer.

That night, the roosters again awoke the Princess. This time, she thought she heard something else. She listened; there was something in the common area. She started to get up, and then decided it must be a guest who had to make use of the facilities. She went back to sleep.

The next morning, she heard much noise and confusion outside her room. Donning her Victoria's Secret robe, she opened her door. There she found a number of guests, along with her fellow volunteers. There had been a break in! A couple from Germany was robbed, and so was the Commoner. The girl's wallet was taken from her backpack, which was right at the foot of her bed. She had not awakened. The thieves cut a screen window and climbed in to the common area.

Apparently they entered the Commoner's room first, then the couple's room, where the husband did wake—he saw two males, and they ran.

That was their first brush with crime in Tonga. The police were notified—they didn't actually come over, but they were notified. The PC required a written report and reimbursed the Commoner for the money taken. Well, as far as the Princess was concerned, certainly not enough to-do had been made. The Queen had insisted on including a small rubber doorstop in her daughter's luggage. The Princess rummaged through her many bags until she found this item. Now, adding to her nightly ritual, after inspecting for spiders, she securely placed it in the crack beneath her door.

By Thursday, one full week had passed since their arrival. The Princess had accumulated a pile of dirty clothes, so she made inquiries as to what to do about laundry, and where to find a Laundromat. She was advised, after trying unsuccessfully to describe to a Tongan what a Laundromat is, that a large plastic bucket and soap is how dirty clothes are dealt with in Tonga. The Princess could not accept this as the final answer to her laundry woes. She expanded her radius of inquiries, and discovered one place that some *palanges* have used to have clothes cleaned. (A palange, she learned, is anyone who is not Polynesian. For example, volunteers from New Zealand, Australia, Japan and America are all classified together as palange.)

The name of this establishment was The Savoy. Armed with directions, she toted a small canvas bag down the street. Within ten minutes, she found The Savoy—however, it was not open. Thinking it was just too early, she sat on the doorstep to wait. It was not long before a Tongan man walked by, nodding and calling out a friendly "malo e lei lei." A few minutes later, he returned.

"Are you waiting for The Savoy?" he asked.

"Io," the Princess answered, proud of herself for responding with the Tongan word for yes. The man informed her that the operators of The Savoy had a death in the family, so they wouldn't be open today. The Princess hauled her bag back to the guesthouse and told her sad story to the others.

The next morning she repeated the process. This time the doors were open. There was a Tongan lady who accepted her bag and placed it on a scale. She informed the Princess that the charge is twenty pa'anga per kilo. This was fine with the Princess, as she needed her clothes clean and this was the only place on the entire island where she could accomplish this goal. She would pay whatever they wanted. The Princess happily made her way to the PC office.

Later, the Dude, the Quiet One and the Duke arrived. They were complaining bitterly that The Savoy was taking advantage of them, that a Tongan would never be charged that much. Apparently, they had decided that the Princess had a good idea, and they took their laundry to The Savoy just after the Princess had left. They had an argument with the lady, and she told them she would ask her boss about the price. The men left her with their laundry and instructions that if it was over ten per kilo not to do it.

The Princess exclaimed, "I hope you didn't include *me* in that!"

"Absolutely," they informed her. "We have a united front, the same price for all volunteers."

The Princess was very upset. She had no intention of scrubbing her clothes in a bucket. An argument ensued.

The lead trainer stepped in. He sent one of the Tongan girls over to The Savoy. She returned with the good news that all PCVs would receive the same price of ten pa'anga per kilo. Another conundrum resolved.

Each day, Group 59 made their way to the office for their ongoing training. Each day, they learned a little bit more about their new home, not just in the classroom, but also through other volunteers already there and exploring the area. There are taxis everywhere, they learned; any ride about town is two pa'anga one-way. The selection of restaurants is rather limited. On the ocean road, about fifteen minutes away from town is the wharf, where small boats sell fresh fish off their decks. Across the street is the Billfish, a small restaurant/bar and the unofficial PC hangout. About a half-block from that is the Waterfront, another bar and restaurant. There is an Italian place called Little Italy, a taxi ride in the opposite direction. Not far from that place is the most expensive restaurant in Tonga, The Sea View, owned and operated by a German couple—this is considered fine dining. Right downtown is a very popular Chinese restaurant Fakalotos. Several months later another place was opened, the Luna Rosa, which was owned and operated by an Italian man married to a Tongan.

That first Friday night in Tonga, Group 59 arrived at the Billfish to discover about a dozen other PCVs already there. A local band was performing live music. They drank, danced, and chatted the night away.

The Princess decided she liked being in the "city." She discreetly investigated how the three other Future Farmers felt about final placement. She was delighted to discover that none of them wished to be placed here. So her mission, and she had decided to accept it, was to make sure that *she* received the Nuku'alofa assignment. This would mean she could remain on Tongatapu and live in or near the capital.

Monday morning, after the prayer, the new recruits were advised on their "home stays," wherein each volunteer would be placed with a Tongan family for the next six weeks training. They would be in the island group of Vava'u, on the second largest island of the country, where there was only one city, Neiafu. The Duke, the Duchess and the Commoner would be in the village called Huoma. The Princess, the Quiet One and the Dude would be in the neighboring village Hakio. Each morning they would be collected and brought to the PC satellite office in downtown Neiafu for training sessions, then returned late afternoon for dinner and evenings with their families. The three younger volunteers didn't have a problem with this, but the Duke, Duchess and Princess were not too happy with the plan. The Princess had lived alone for a long time—she wouldn't want to live with her own family for six weeks, much less with strangers.

They were informed that this system would provide a cultural awareness that could not be received any other way. The home stay would only be for six weeks; besides, all houses were within walking distance of each other.

They were to leave for the island of Vava'u the next day. They were told to go through their belongings to take what they would need for the next six weeks, and that anything else could be stored at the PC headquarters. They were to be at the office by 2:00 p.m.

The Princess sifted through her three extra-large duffel bags, her one medium duffle bag, her carryon, her backpack and her bike. She rearranged, eliminated and selected the necessary items for the next six weeks. She took one extra-large duffle bag and her backpack; everything else she stored.

Everyone arrived at the office. They all piled into the PC van and were taken to the wharf, where they discovered a cargo ship. This giant freighter was painted a bright orange, with the name *Ola' Vaha* on the side.

They were given tickets; they boarded the ship, along with about 150 Tongans. The ship was not set up for passengers, even though it was obvious that carrying passengers in addition to freight was the norm and not the exception—there were no seats, benches or chairs. There were three levels. The Tongans with crates of live pigs and chickens stayed on the first level. The volunteers made their way to the second level, where they staked out a small area for themselves on the cold steel floor. They were back away from the railing with the added protection of the level above providing a roof.

The volunteers made themselves as comfortable as possible using their duffle bags and backpacks. The ship was to set sail at 5:00 p.m. and arrive in Neiafu at 11:00 a.m. the next day. They prepared themselves for what they expected to be about the most boring eighteen hours of their lives. Ha! They had no idea!

The freighter glided out of the dock and headed out to sea. The many people on the ship were talking, laughing and getting settled down. People, including the volunteers, opened bags of food and drink they had brought along. The sun went down; people fell asleep. As the ship steamed through the ocean, everything was quiet.

About two in the morning, the weather started picking up. The ship rocked slightly from side to side. The *Ola' Vaha* was a very large cargo ship, but the Pacific Ocean is larger. The weather got worse and pretty soon the freighter was bobbing around like a cork. People started to wake up.

A few start hanging over the railing feeding the fish. Soon there were dozens of people clinging to the rail. The people on the top deck were being violently ill overboard also, the effects of which rained down onto the second level.

The Princess knew what was to come. She could feel herself getting ill, but could not bring herself to vomit over the side in front of all these people. She decided to make a dash for the toilets located inside the ship. The ship was rocking so much that she was "pinballed" from side to side along her route. She thought she would not make it, when a starboard lurch threw her through the bathroom door. Another lurch, this time to port, brought her to her knees in front of the toilet just in the nick of time. The Princess made her deposit. Again the ship lurched to the right, sloshing everything out of the toilet all over the Princess. That was so repulsive that she vomited again, and again her input was output all over her. This cycle repeated itself several times before she could throw herself away from the commode, grab onto the sink and pull herself to her feet.

Facing her, above the basin, was her reflection. What a sight to behold! Her face and sweatshirt were covered with vomit! In her hair were the undigested chunks of food. Oh my God! How was this to be endured? The paper towel dispenser was empty. She tried the faucet—there was water flowing from the tap. She splashed water onto her face. It was then that the Princess realized, this too she would survive. All was not lost, at least not her sense of humor. She leaned forward and whispered, "Mirror, mirror on the wall…who's the fairest of them all?"

Checking her plastic digital watch, she discovered it was only 3:00 a.m. The destination was still eight hours away.

Home: 1. A house or other place of residence. 2. The place in which one's domestic affections are centered.

Stay: 1. To remain in a place, condition or situation. 2. To live or dwell. 3. To be steadfast or persevere.

Household: 1. The people of a house collectively.

Love: 1. A profoundly, tender, passionate affection for another person. 2. An intense personal attachment.

Shack: 1. A crudely built hut, cabin, or house.

HOMESTAY

The bedraggled volunteers finally arrived at the dock in Vava'u, where Peace Corps picked them up. The group was exhausted from their tribulation. The drive to the neighboring villages of Huoma and Hakio lasted twenty minutes.

This island is quite different from the main island, Tongatapu, which is totally flat and densely populated; its capital city, Nuku'alofa, is home to thirty thousand people. The island of Vava'u, on the other hand, is covered with small rolling hills, heavily cultivated land, and acres of crops, with almost no houses visible from the main road. The only city, Neiafu, was an intersection of two streets, with all of the island businesses: a bank, several small groceries, the tourist office, a small department store and a video rental, with the Peace Corps satellite office down the road.

The Peace Corps minivan stopped first in Hakio, a very tiny village of no more than two dozen homes. The first stop was the Dude's new temporary home. Several small children ran out to escort him to the door. The house across the street from this was the Princess's home stay. This was painted a peeling pink and turquoise with "LOVE SHACK" printed on the sloped roof. Our Princess gave the Duchess a "What do you think that means?" look. The Duchess whispered in reply, "Don't worry, we will come and find you as soon as we get settled."

The Princess knocked on the door. When she received no answer, she knocked again.... Still, she did not receive a response. Meanwhile, the van had deposited the Quiet One at a house down the dirt road behind the Princesses.

As the van returned past the Princess to continue on to Huoma, the driver stopped and one of the Tongan trainers got out. He also knocked on the door, then opened and called inside, "Malo e lei lei." Still there was no response. The two entered the house; no one was home. The Princess was instructed to remain at the house; after the rest of the group was taken to their home stays, the trainer would return and locate a member of the family. She was left alone.

She was standing inside the front door, which opened into a large room with a wooden bench along one wall. There was no other furniture, but she saw many straw mats rolled up in a corner. To the right was a bedroom. Straight ahead was a very small room with a couch and an easy chair covered by sheets, with a coffee table in front. There was a television and a VCR atop a large square table. This was encouraging. Connected to this room was another bedroom containing a double bed and a chest of drawers. When she returned to the front door, she continued the other way. She found a kitchen with a wooden picnic table and benches, a small refrigerator, and cast iron burners connected to a propane tank next to a sink.

Investigating further, she passed through the kitchen and discovered a wooden door that opened to a cement shower stall containing a three-foot square open space where a window should be—but there was no glass. Hmm, the Princess noticed, this open space is chest high—if you were showering you would be clearly visible. She noticed there was only one faucet.

Peering behind a plastic shower curtain hanging next to the shower was the dirtiest commode she had ever encountered! Retreating once again to the front door, she observed one more tiny bedroom.

After her ordeal on the Ola' Vaha, the Princess desperately wanted a hot shower and a change to clean clothes. She now realized that was not going to happen, as the single faucet seemed to indicate no hot water.

The Princess returned to the TV room. She shook out the sheet on the couch to see just what it covered, at the same time checking for bugs. Satisfied with what she saw she replaced the sheet and perched on the edge of the sofa.

Before long, she heard an engine. The trainer had returned, followed by another car. The man driving the second car hopped out and rushed to the door. His name was Havea, her homestay father. He was very apologetic that no one had been here to greet her. His wife's sister had died suddenly, so his wife had gone to Hai'pai for the funeral. Everyone else in the family was at work. He begged her to make herself at home. The Princess assured Havea she would be fine, so he could feel free to return to work.

Once again she was left alone. Not knowing what room would be hers, she could not unpack. The time was only 1:30 in the afternoon, and she knew of no better way to kill time than to read. Taking her book from her backpack, she again lay on the sheet-covered couch. Soon, her exhaustion overtook her, and she fell asleep.

Hearing someone calling her name, the Princess jerked awake, for a moment forgetting where she was. She rushed outside—the Duke and the Duchess had found her! The Duke suggested she walk with them to their village to learn the way.

The trio set off through the center of the village, taking a different route from the way the Duke and the Duchess had come. Any Tongans they saw waved and called "malo e lei lei." They smiled and waved back. At the edge of town the dirt road was no longer hard packed, and became muddy, the rich clay soil clinging to their sandals. Soon, the only way the Princess could pull her foot from the suction was to grab behind her knee with both hands and yank, freeing first one foot and then the other. Before long, the threesome were all up to their ankles in ooze. Oh, this is really too much, thought the Princess. Her $150 Timberland flip-flops were completely submerged. The essence of vomit still clung to her clothing. She felt like she was on the verge of a crying jag, when, suddenly, the Duchess exploded with laughter. The Duke and the Princess exchanged a look. The Duke demanded, "What is so funny?"

The Duchess was doubled over with glee. Gasping for breath, she exclaimed, "If the people back home could see us now." She was contagious. Standing there stuck in the middle of the road, all three found their ridiculous situation side-splitting.

The Princess took the original, dry route her friends had used to make her way "home."

Her new family began arriving shortly after 5:00 p.m. With Havea, the father she had already met, was the teenage daughter, Emelina. The oldest daughter, Lesieli, and her husband, Samuela, were introduced. They had with them their two-year-old son, Isi, and the 12-year-old brother, Nisilli. This was everyone, with the exception of the mother, also named Emelina. There was a slight language problem. They understood a lot of English but not all. The Princess spoke almost no Tongan. This was a learning experience for all.

The Princess settled in to her new home. Each morning she would arise about 7:30. Her family would provide bread and butter for breakfast. Emelina would go outside and reappear with a pitcher of water, which she placed on the table. The Princess had no idea where this water came from, but she knew it was not the bottled water she purchased in Nuku'alofa. Not wishing to offend, she didn't ask where it came from, but drank just enough to wash the bread down.

They all would take turns using the cement shower. Showering required a slight squatting to not be revealed through the open window. The chill of the morning air, combined with the icy water from the showerhead, took her breath away. No matter what anyone said, the Princess knew that roosters and cold showers were two things she would never become accustomed to.

Then the Princess would dress for the day. In Nuku'alofa she had purchased a number of lovely hand-painted sarongs, so she could be attired appropriately daily. Each day, the PC van would retrieve the group at about 9:00 a.m. for classes. The mornings consisted of three hours of language, and the afternoons of cultural issues and of preparation for a small business workshop they would present to a local youth group.

Each evening, dinner was prepared and placed on the table for the Princess. After she had eaten, then the family would get together and eat. She found this odd—she tried to encourage them all to eat together, but two things happened to show her the wisdom of this method. First, Isi, the two year-old, had a habit of removing all his clothes and running around naked. She observed him peeing out the back door onto the dog, then climbing up to the kitchen table and grabbing himself a handful of whatever was there. Having witnessed Isi previously grabbing a handful of himself, the Princess would prefer to dine *before* he did. Second, she ascertained, she was given all the food first so she could choose what she liked and they could eat what she left. Since the Princess did not care for most of the traditional Tongan food—*ufi, manioki,* or *taro*—there was always plenty left.

Her family showed concern for how little she ate. The unrealistic figure all women in America aspire to—the incredibly thin, shapeless form of a model, albeit impossible to maintain and unthinkably unhealthy—is unknown to Tongans. They saw her as someone sickly who needed to be fattened up. Soon they discovered the only thing they could get the Princess to eat was potatoes and chicken. So they offered this to her nightly. During her home stay, the Princess did lose twelve pounds!

It was a status symbol in Tonga to have a PCV staying in your home. Others in the village had loaned her family the use of the TV and VCR in the Princess's honor.

That first Saturday, Lesieli returned from a cousin's home very excited. She had procured, for the weekend, an electric sandwich maker. The whole family was thrilled.

Everyone gathered in the kitchen as Lesieli made the first sandwich. It was presented to the Princess. On the plate in front of her sat two triangles of bread with the middle crimped closed. The Princess wondered what could be inside the sealed bread.

Surrounding her were the laughing, happy faces of this family that had taken her into their home, waiting expectantly for her to sample her sandwich. She picked up one half and bit into it. As she pulled the balance of the bread away from her mouth, she could see soft, white, round threads extending from the other half with a red liquid oozing out. Oh my God, she thought, they have fed me worms! Everyone was clapping and calling out "*ifo*," the Tongan word for delicious. She was able to swallow the bite whole. Afraid to ask, but more afraid not to, she inquired, "Ko e hau," meaning "What." Not having the words to translate, Emelina grabbed from the counter a tin can. The red and yellow label clearly stated, Franco American Spaghetti. Joining the laughter, she exclaimed with much enthusiasm, "Ifo, ifo alpeito!"—"Very delicious!"—and gobbled up the entire thing. She learned from other volunteers later that one can is rather pricey. The Tongans feel Franco American Spaghetti is a rare treat. This had never been on a list of items that the Princess considered culinary delights, but nothing had ever tasted so good!

Our Princess learned many things during her home stay. She learned about different types of food, how to burn trash, and trying out a new language. She learned that the children all call their parents by their first name, instead of Mom and Dad. Most of all, she learned that sisters are sisters, no matter what country you are in. Lesieli made the Princess a handbag woven out of frond strips. Delighted, the Princess presented Lesieli with a bottle of shower gel, knowing that cosmetics and toiletries are difficult to come by here in Tonga. Leisieli made the Princess swear not to tell her younger sister Emelina of this gift. Emelina offered to teach the Princess how to weave a fan; in return the Princess gave her matching nail polish and lipstick, to which Emelina extracted a solemn oath of secrecy from the Princess. The Princess also learned that nothing is owned; there is no "mine" or "yours"; everything is communal. Each dress, kia-kia, pair of flip-flops, down to the hair ribbon, "belongs" to whoever puts it on first that day. Knowing this, the Princess was in complete understanding of the girls tucking away the tiny treats they received.

After the Princess pulled a deck of playing cards from her backpack, Nisilli challenged her nightly to a game of *Sweepy*, the Tongan version of War. The twelve-year-old brother spoke the best English in the family, and he was tireless in his efforts to defeat the Princess again and again. However, the continual thrashings did help her learn her numbers. In Tongan, there are the numbers zero through ten. Any numbers larger than ten, you put two numbers together: for example, instead of saying twelve you said, one-two or for forty-five you would say four-five—what could be simpler?

The home stay was better than she had expected. Still, for her as a city girl, Hakio was way, way too rural for the Princess, with one notable exception—no roosters. There was however, the church bell.

Every morning, except Saturday, the church bell rang. Sort of a village-wide alarm clock, it was very effective! What appeared to be a replica of the Liberty Bell was suspended in a wooden tower, dangling from a long rope. This rope was pulled approximately seventy to eighty times at 5:00 a.m. This was the wake-up call. At 5:30 a.m., there was a loud prolonged ringing of the bell. This meant, "Hurry up." At 6:00 a.m., the bell tolled, "We're starting without you." This was repeated at 5:00 p.m. for the evening service. You didn't have to get there on time, but you had to make an appearance. The local boys usually showed up for the last twenty minutes.

On her first Sunday in Hakio, the Princess took out her most expensive sarong. She matched the soft, pastel shades of the wrap with a pink cotton blouse. Slipping into color-coordinated pink Lands' End flip-flops, she thought she looked quite fetching.

Havea, her "father," took one look at her and left the room. A few minutes later, Emelina came in to inform the Princess, "We dress up for church." The Princess was slightly offended, thinking, I *am* dressed up!

Emelina and Leseili joined forces to appropriately attire her. They tied a white bed sheet around her waist; according to the girls, having a flash of white showing around the ankles is very elegant. Next, the older sister graciously loaned the Princess a multi-layered, ruffled, bright red and yellow dress. As Leseili had about ninety pounds on the Princess, the American woman now felt like that can of Franco American Spaghetti. Wait, they were not finished yet. No "Sunday-go-to-meetin'" outfit was complete without the talvala. They honored her with the loan of their most formal version: they tied on her a straw floor mat, which extended from chest to lower calves. The girls admired their creation: *Now* she is dressed up! Well, what is a Princess to do? she thought. She didn't want to insult her "family." Besides, she thought, who is going to see me? Off they went, arm in arm, to the church. When she entered, who did she see sitting in the back row but the Dude and the Quiet One! She saw them elbowing each other and placing their hands over their mouths. As she passed down the aisle, they could barely contain the snickers. How mortifying!

After church, each family had the traditional umu, cooking in a pit in the yard, then had naptime. Havea slept on a mat in the main room. Nisilli and Isi curled up together, asleep on the couch. The others retired to bedrooms. The Princess quietly snuck out and made her way over to Huoma. She found the Duke and the Duchess on the front porch of their home stay. The Duchess displayed the hideous contraption she was required to wear to the service. Even the Princess had to agree that the Duchess's attire was worse that what she had endured. They vowed not to go through this same thing again. Before the next Sunday, they would buy a Tongan dress, of their choosing, in their own size; and forget the talvala, a kia-kia would be acceptable.

Then the Duchess described her breakfast experience. She had requested a hard-boiled egg, feeling this would be the safest, since it is cooked in its own shell. One of the children collected some eggs from the back yard. They were popped into a pot of water, poop and all, to boil. Then, her home stay mother removed the eggs and poured that water into a coffee cup for the Duchess's coffee!

The Commoner made an appearance at their little gathering. She was outfitted in a Tongan dress her home stay mother had made for her.

"That is adorable!" the Duchess exclaimed.

"I *know*! I loved it so much, she made me three more," the Commoner explained. "Isn't it great?"

"So, everything is going well with your home stay?" asked the Princess.

"Not exactly. There are six little children and they are really cute; I love them, but they want to sit on me and play with my hair. Which would be okay, but they all have lice and now I think I have lice," she complained.

"Oh my God!" gasped the Princess "What do you do about that?"

The Commoner replied, "The PCMO said she will give me a special shampoo, but then I have to get all the kids to use it too, or we'll just trade the lice back and forth. Anyway, I spoke to Drew and I requested to be sent up to the Niuas."

"What?!" both women exclaimed, astounded. "There is no electricity or running water! And no flush toilet!"

"I know," the younger girl responded, "but I feel this will be the 'real' Peace Corps experience."

The Duchess and the Princess looked at each other and agreed that their experience had already been "real" enough for them.

The next week, the Princess learned that Leseili's birthday was coming up. She also learned that the traditional Tonga birthday celebration was simply, "The family says an extra prayer for you." Well, the Princess took it upon herself to share an American experience with her family, so she got from the PC staff the name of a Tongan lady who would make a cake for ten pa'anga.

On the appointed day, the Princess got a ride to pick up the cake. Along the route home, the van stopped for her to purchase ice cream. Her family was ecstatic when she presented the ice cream and cake and sang "Happy Birthday." No one ate any dinner that night. They divided the cake and ice cream immediately, and consumed the entire thing!

The next week, the Princess was informed that Nisilli had a birthday. She repeated the process for him. The week after was Havea's birthday. Amazingly, every member of her home stay family had a birthday in the six weeks she was there!

Right outside the Love Shack, practically in the front yard, was what was known as the Phone Booth. This was a tiny wooden hut that contained the one phone in the village. Each household contributed a few pa'anga each month to employ several young girls to man the booth from 9:00 a.m. to 10:00 p.m. When a call came in, the girl on duty would hail anyone within shouting distance to run over and tell so and so that they got a call. Calls could also be placed from this phone booth.

The phone booth was the hangout for all the unmarried girls of the village. Many nights the Princess would join Emelina to socialize at the phone booth.

"Where are the boys? Why don't they hang out here at the phone booth with you girls?" questioned the Princess.

This remark was met with much giggling. "The boys gather at the town hall," one of the girls informed her.

"Well," the Princess said, "in America, wherever the young girls are the young boys follow." When the only response was blushes accompanying more giggling she continued. "How do you get dates if the boys are always in one place and you in another?"

One girl asked, "What is a date?"

"What's a date!" the Princess could not believe her ears. "That's when the boy borrows his father's car, picks you up and takes you to dinner or a movie, sometimes both."

This really drove the girls wild with glee. They hugged each other and laughed till they cried.

"An unmarried girl can never be alone with a boy," one youth said to enlighten her.

Another added, "If a boy likes you, he asks your father if you can be the *to'a* for a kava party."

"If your father approves, he holds a kava party at your home and all the men sit in one room on the mats and you get to be the one preparing and passing the kava," said yet another, continuing her education. "Your mother and sisters are in the next room and they listen. If the boy and girl like each other, you do this again and again."

"If your families both approve, then you can get married," another supplied.

"I think singing practice is the best way to be with boys," remarked Emelina.

"Tell me about that," requested the Princess.

"Several evening a week, there is singing practice at the church," she explained. "The young people all get together and sing for a few hours, with chaperones, of course. Then we walk home together in a group."

This is dating Tongan Style.

Late one afternoon, the Duchess stopped at the Princess's house on her way back from town with a package that had arrived at the PC office for the Princess. The two opened the package on the front porch. Inside were four cartons of the Princess's cherished cigarettes, gum, magazines and several bags of candy. When her home stay sisters came out to the patio, the Princess held out a bag of candy. "Would you like some?" she asked.

The girls grabbed the bag from her. Calling out "malo alpieto," they ran to the phone booth.

The Princess looked at the Duchess. "What just happened here?" she queried.

"Your sisters just ran off with your whole bag of candy!" she laughed. "I had the same thing happen to me with a bag of potato chips. I think we're missing something."

Besides the cultural differences that arose, there were several routine facts of life that presented a problem. The Princess needed a haircut. Her close-cropped hair had grown out, no longer appearing to have any style at all. In addition, her feet were a mess. Wearing nothing but a variety of flip-flops had exposed her tender appendages to the elements. She commiserated with the Duchess.

One problem was quickly solved: the Duchess knew how to cut hair. Getting out her special scissors, she dragged a plastic chair outside, wrapped a towel around the Princess's shoulders and went to work. Wow! The Princess was thrilled with the results.

When the Princess returned to her home stay family, Emelina noticed the new do. She remarked how she would love to lose her long and heavy locks. This surprised the Princess—because her thin, baby fine hair had always been her biggest cosmetic problem, she was in awe of the Tongans' beautiful mane. Emelina pointed out how incredibly *hot* such thick hair can be. Well then, why doesn't she cut it? No, the girl, sadly shakes her head, her father would never approve. What does Havea have to do with Emelina getting a hair cut? Once more, she was enlightened: no girl, or for that matter, woman, can get a haircut without the permission of her father or her husband. The Princess wisely kept her thoughts about this tradition to herself.

The girl's foot problems were not so easily satisfied. Combining their efforts, they displayed and compared the utensils available to them. They added heated water to a soapy bucket and took turns soaking their tootsies. Then after much scraping and scrubbing, they applied petroleum jelly and covered their feet with clean soft cotton socks. In twenty-four hours, they vowed, they would check the results.

Another vanity that the Princess maintained in her Tongan home was using her tiny dryer to style her hair. The large mirror in the front room was the best place for her daily ritual. On one such occasion, out from behind the looking glass emerged a colossal spider! The Princess shrieked helplessly. Her father, Havea, and Leseili dashed to her side, wondering whatever could be the problem.

The Princess pointed to the offending arachnid. The two looked back and forth from the wall to the Princess, clearly not comprehending the situation. "Oh, kill it! Kill it!" she wailed.

Once they understand her desire, they were stupefied! Havea exited the room. His daughter looked at the Princess in amazement. "Kill the spider?" she asked. "The spider is good! The spider saved the baby Jesus!"

What??!! Our Princess did know a bit about the Bible. Her paternal grandparents were Southern Baptists. In her youth, she and her brother had spent time with them every summer. They each were supplied with a Bible with their name monogrammed in gold on the cover. Bible-reading time was required before playtime. She had read the entire book, more than once! "How did the spider save the baby Jesus?" she asked.

Displaying much compassion for the Princess's ignorance, Leseili explained. "The king's men were killing all the babies. Jesus was hidden in a cave and the spider spun a web over the entrance. When the king's men saw the web was not disturbed, they passed by that cave!"

This sounds like something from a Cecil B. DeMille movie, thought the Princess. And she did not want to debate religion with a Tongan. However, she simply could not cohabitate with this creature. Finally, Leseili scooped him up and threw him outside.

Meanwhile, it was time for the volunteers to hold a three-day small business workshop. Thirty Tongan youth were expected at the PC office in downtown Neiafu. The volunteers had divided the days up into sections. Each person was to lead a ninety-minute session. The first day the Quiet One started off. He had already mastered enough Tongan that he gave a great deal of his presentation in the native tongue. The Duke spoke entirely in English but held their interest, as it was still the first day.

The second day the youth were not as enthusiastic. It was a struggle to understand everything in a second language. In addition, the room was very warm. The

Princess was to take her turn after lunch. While everyone was eating, she got an idea. She hurried the few blocks from the PC office to town. She purchased several bags of small wrapped candies. Her presentation was about the steps to take before you open a small business. She wanted to engage the youth, for them to join in, to participate and not just listen to a lecture.

She started by writing the word "IDEAS" on the blackboard, and asked for someone to translate that to Tongan. When someone did, she tossed him a piece of candy. She requested people to call out any idea for a business. She tossed a piece of candy to each person who tossed out an idea. Soon, candy and ideas started flying across the room. The blackboard was full. She was able to maintain their interest throughout her presentation.

After the success of the workshop, the volunteers went to one of the two bars for a celebratory drink. A number of the volunteers that lived on the island were there as well.

At the bar was a married couple that had only been in Tonga a few months. They had quite an interesting story. The duo started their PC service in the Solomon Islands. They had completed the training program and been sworn in. Roughly six months later, civil unrest broke out in the country. All PCVs in the Solomons were instructed to "stand down" this, meaning they could not leave their site, or house. Then they were told to pack up all their belonging with their address in the States clearly marked outside the box. In addition, they had to keep a backpack containing any valuables ready to go at a moment's notice. They stayed in this stressful state for quite some time, with little or no contact with other volunteers. All of a sudden, the PC van showed up at their house, loaded them in and whisked them to the airport. Here, they finally connected with their friends. The volunteers were evacuated to Vanuatu. They waited there for a week to see if things calmed down in the Solomons.

Then Washington PC made the decision that it was too dangerous to return. Volunteers within months of completing their service were sent home. Other countries nearby were contacted to see if they could accept any additional recruits. Kiribas, Samoa, Tonga and Vanuatu all were accommodating to the now homeless ones. Five were sent to Tonga. They expressed great sadness at not being able to say goodbye to the locals they had worked with and become close to. They still have no word on the belongings they abandoned. They now had to forget the new language they had learned and learn another.

The Peace Corps had no choice—they could not risk volunteers being injured, killed or held hostage. Everyone agreed, the correct action had been taken. Wow, what an exciting tale!

In addition to having several drinks, the Princess ordered a pizza to take home with her. She was really looking forward to this! Her family was all in the TV room watching a movie. She dropped the foil wrapped treasure on the coffee table and made use of the nasty, dirty toilet. When she returned, the six had divided the pizza amongst themselves and were tickled to death with what they obviously thought was a treat she had brought for them! The Princess received nothing but the mouth-watering smell.

At some point during the training process, the CD and Drew, the APCD, made the trip to the Niua Islands. The only access to these two remote islands was the small plane that made the trip each Friday, weather permitting. If the winds were high or the climate stormy, the plane did not take the risk. Travelers were likely to get stuck up there for several weeks, simply to avoid a disastrous return flight.

The two were scheduled to go on a Friday morning and planned on returning the next Friday. The purpose of their visit was to approve a site and establish interest in the Future Farmers of the Pacific program. It looked like the Commoner could get her wish for the "real" PC experience here, as there would be no electricity, no running water and no flush toilet.

This was encouraging to the Princess; maybe she could obtain her goal, to be placed in the capital, Nuku'alofa.

With two weeks of training left, the Princess's home stay "mother," named Emelina like the daughter, returned from Hai'pai. She was a very sweet and friendly woman. However, she spoke no English at all, therefore the only way they could communicate was through the other members of the family. She was a master weaver. Night after night, she sat cross-legged on a straw mat with strips of fronds and created a masterpiece. Nisilli had to find a new Sweepy partner, as the mother and two sisters spent their evenings together teaching the Princess the age-old tradition.

During the last week, real problems developed. The four volunteers participating in the Future Farmers of the Pacific were called into the PC office. The funding had not come through for the start-up of the new program. In addition, it appeared the cart had been put before the horse as far as marketing goes. There was nothing to market.

The Future Farmers of the Pacific would have to begin at the beginning—meaning, these volunteers would all be village-based, where they would need to create a youth group, gathering together any unemployed youth into a cohesive organization. The volunteers would have to secure farmland, plan what to plant, how much and when to harvest. Then they would have something to sell.

The Quiet One was the first to voice his disapproval. He had been an agricultural volunteer in Africa, so had specifically chosen this program for the marketing aspect. This was shaping up as nothing but a village youth worker—not what he signed up for.

The Princess was devastated. She too complained. She had asked very direct questions, about this exact thing, of the country desk in D.C. before accepting this assignment. She had been assured this was a marketing position.

The CD reminded her that this was the PC, and a volunteer must be flexible. She assured him that she is quite *flexible*, but not qualified to go out in the bush and teach the youth of Tonga about crop rotation!

The Dude was completely fine with the way things were. Being a happy-go-lucky young man, he readily agreed to whatever was needed.

The Commoner was also content with the adjustment to the program, as long as she could remain in Vava'u. She had decided that the little city of Neiafu was to her liking. This was where she needed to be placed. *What?* Everyone was astounded. She had been whining for weeks about the "real" PC experience.

The CD and Drew had gone to a great deal of trouble to develop a site in the Niuas specifically because the Commoner had requested this location. The country director himself promised that a volunteer would be sent there within the month.

The CD displayed his own reaction to their reactions. He was furious. After making his thoughts crystal clear to the foursome—*he* is the *boss*, *he* is the one who tells you what you will or will not do, and *he* is the *country director, God damn it*! And, you will do *exactly* what *he* says or you will be on the next plane—he stormed out of the office.

The Princess fled to the bosom of her best friends. The Duke and the Duchess were having dinner with their APCD, the woman in charge of the education side of PC Tonga. They invited her to join them; maybe the Protector could be of assistance.

During dinner the Princess sobbed out her sad story. The Protector immediately assuaged her fears. She agreed with the Princess that this project was not the job for her, and pointed out that Tonga has many needs for PCVs in a number of capacities. She promised that she would get together with Drew to see what they could work out.

The two boys, the Dude and the Quiet One, were upset, too, especially with the Commoner. With her backing out on the Niuas, they feared one of them would be sent there. Neither one relished the idea of having to live for two years with a latrine, no electricity or running water. This was not a location in the original program. It had been pledged only because of her request.

Only a few days before the swearing in, which would make them official Peace Corps volunteers, Drew had a conference with each one individually. He advised them of the CDs final decision.

The Commoner was first; she was called into a small room at the office. The other three were sitting right outside smoking. They realized they could hear everything going on inside. The Quiet One walked away. The Princess and the Dude eavesdropped. The Commoner was informed that she was going to the Niua Islands. She had requested this and they had gone to a great deal of trouble to secure it for her. That was to be her post. The Princess peered over the windowsill in time to see the Commoner prostrate herself on the table and sob.

The APCD sat there unmoved. In a few minutes the young girl got up and exited the building, walking past the two standing there without saying a word.

The Dude was next. He was being sent to Hai'pai. He was very happy.

Next, it was the Princess's turn. She was being placed here in Vava'u. Housing was difficult to come by on this island. The CD had secured her a room in a house that she would share with two Tongan nurses. He thought that this would be a good experience for her.

The Princess responded, "Fat chance!"

Enough was enough. She was no longer in control of her life. She was told what to eat and when to eat it, what to wear and when to wear it, how to act and when to act that way. She felt she had been sufficiently agreeable, adaptable, and affable.

She had something to say. Number one, she complained, every other volunteer has his or her own house. She refuses to do a two-year home stay, which is basically what they are saying. Number two, she is not qualified for this position.

She informed Mr. Havea, she wants to stay in Tonga, and she believes she has something to offer. She has a business background; tourism experience and the entrepreneurial spirit—there must be another place for her here.

He quietly suggested to the Princess that she accept what was offered for now, for her to get sworn in and become an official volunteer. He and the Protector would work behind the scenes to find something else. The CD would be finished with his tour in eight weeks; after he left they could place her wherever they wanted.

The Princess quickly processed this data. Okay.

Lastly, the Quiet One was informed he would be placed in Nuku'alofa. He would be working side by side with Drew and the ministries of Tonga. He would be the project leader for the program, in charge of organizing the entire operation, and would be the liaison with the project leader in Samoa.

So, the day before swearing in, this was how it stood:

The Quiet One was to be placed in Tongatapu.

The Princess was to stay in Vava'u.

The Dude was to move to Hai'pai.

The Commoner was to be sent to the Niua's.

Swear-in: 1. To bind oneself by an oath. 2. To make a solemn declaration. 3. To admit to office by administering an oath.

Official: 1. A person holding an office or charges with certain duties. 2. Appointed or authorized by a government or organization. 3. Public and formal.

Volunteer: 1. A person who voluntarily offers himself or herself for a service or undertaking. 2. To offer, give or perform voluntarily.

SWEARING-IN

The Peace Corps swearing-in ceremony is a big deal. This was an official commitment the volunteers were making, a promise, a solemn vow. In addition, this was the grand opening of the Vava'u Youth Computer Center, just added to the Neiafu PC office. A room with eight computers, it was the first of its kind in Vava'u for the youth to have access and instruction on word processing, the Internet and the like.

The Tongan trainers spent the day decorating the outside of the Neiafu Peace Corps office. They placed palm fronds and flowers around every pillar and post. A small tent was set up for the CD and the special guests: the governor of Vava'u, the head minister of the Free Wesleyan Church and from Peace Corps Washington, and the regional director of the Inter-America and Pacific Region. This regional director (RD) would perform the actual swearing-in. Several rows of folding chairs were placed along the right side of the yard for the new volunteers and their "families." On the opposite side of the yard were straw mats for current volunteers and any other guests.

Emelina, the Princess's mother, sent Nisilli and her daughter, Emelina, out to the fields for flowers and a special type of berry. She stayed up late into the night creating a very special *sia-sia*. This is a form of the kia-kia, but made of all fresh leaves and blossoms.

It is made as close to the event as possible. This is a great honor. This is worn in place of the straw kia-kia over the traditional Tongan dress.

The Princess was distraught. She was bewildered. She was agitated. Should she or should she not go through with the ceremony? What if the Protector and Drew could not relocate her? She felt as if she were about to get married to a man she wasn't sure if she loved. She had two choices. One, she could quit now and go home, which to her was out of the question. Two, she could commit herself as a volunteer and hope for the best.

The festivities were scheduled to begin at 4:00 p.m. There was an official welcoming of the guests with speeches by a number of people—long-winded speeches, all in Tongan—followed by a few hymns and a prayer. After that a youth group performed a musical number.

Finally, the big moment: the RD made another speech. Then he raised his right hand, as did the Princess and her five companions. And so, with a few "I solemnly swears" they were official Peace Corps volunteers.

After the ceremony there was a barbecue for everyone. The CD came over to the Princess; he told her he was glad she had come to her senses and accepted his advice. He knew she would be grateful in the future. It would have been a shame for him to have had to send her home just because she was so stubborn. A hot retort came to the Princess's lips, when once again, she heard the Queen's voice, "If you can't say anything nice, say nothing at all." The Princess presented him her back and walked away. By 5:30 p.m. it was all over.

This night was for them to celebrate. The Princess did not feel like celebrating. After changing into American clothes, she did go with the Duke and the Duchess out for a drink.

Upon entering the establishment, they immediately spied the CD with the RD at a table. Before they could retreat, they were spotted. The CD jumped up and waved them over. There was no escape; the three were forced to sit down with the CD and RD for a drink.

This was the first time they had chatted with the RD. He asked them where they were from, their backgrounds, etc. Then to their astonishment he told them that statistically, "older volunteers had little or no chance of completing their service." He went on to say that "older" volunteers just could not adjust to the poor living conditions, the frustrations, and the lack of instant success.

The Duke was incensed. First of all, he wanted to know what "statistics" were these? How long had there been "older" volunteers and what was the ratio, old to young? Second, he demanded to know why would the PC accept "older" volunteers if this was true? Third, why the hell did this man fly halfway around the world to swear in three people he felt were doomed?

The RD informed them that he didn't fly here to swear them in, he just happened to be visiting this region at this time. The PC couldn't discriminate against the "elderly."

Elderly! The three were forty-five, fifty, and fifty-five years old—hardly *elderly*!

The Duke turned to the girls, "I think we should be getting home."

"Absolutely," said the Princess. She jumped up from the table, inadvertently tipping her glass of white wine right in the RD's lap.

The Duke remarked, "Hope that isn't your only suit. But maybe now you can be culturally sensitive and wear the tupano and the talvala."

The indignant threesome stormed out.

"How did he ever get such an important job?" asked the Duchess. "He knows nothing about what we have to go through! He should have been required to have been a volunteer. How dare he tell us we will fail, hours after he swore us in? I nearly died when you spilled your drink on him!"

"That was an accident!" exclaimed the Princess. "I don't understand why he would tell us that even if it was true."

"That is an appointed position by the current administration," the Duke informed them.

"Hope he has his résumé in order. He will be pounding the pavement in January. That reminds me, our absentee ballots should be in Nuku'alofa by now."

The next morning they were all taken to the tiny airstrip for the flight to Nuku'alofa. Thank God they did not have to return the way they came, on the Ola' Vaha.

There was, however, the humiliation of each person publicly being weighed to stabilize the small aircraft. As all watched, one by one, the passengers stepped on the giant scale.

Then one airline employee shouted to another the amount, in the Princess's case, "Seventy kilos."

"Now, wait just a minute!" exclaimed the Princess. "I have my shoes on, and my backpack is quite heavy! I do not weigh seventy kilos!"

"You taking your shoes and backpack on the plane?"

"Well, yes!"

"Seventy kilos. *Next!*"

At least it is in kilos, thought the Princess. A little math is required to convert this to pounds.

Finally, with all twenty-four travelers balanced in their designated seats, they departed Neiafu, Vava'u.

RETURN TO NUKU'ALOFA

Returning to Nuku'alofa, the six newly sworn-in volunteers were deposited back at the same guesthouse. The Duke and the Duchess stayed in the same room they had been in previously, on the second floor. The Princess claimed the only other room upstairs next to them. The Quiet One, the Dude and the Commoner were on the first floor.

The Duchess and the Princess immediately noticed how much better the accommodations were. Wow, this place has really been fixed up, they commented. They marveled at the change. It was cleansed. It was purified. It was decontaminated!

The Duke, however, was not impressed. He advised the ladies, "This place is exactly the same as it was. Your frame of reference is what has changed. After the home stays, this is like the Taj Mahal."

They arrived on Wednesday afternoon, and the Dude and the Commoner had a week and a half to determine what they needed to take with them to their islands. They would depart the following Friday. The Dude would be shipped a propane stove/oven and a small electric refrigerator. The Commoner would be shipped a propane stove/oven only, as of course there would be no electricity where she was going.

The Duke and the Duchess would move into their new abode, a short bike ride away, on Friday.

A house had not yet been secured for the Quiet One; it was still being debated which village he would be placed in.

The Princess, Drew and the Protector were on a quest to find her another position before the CD caught on to them.

Limbo: 1. A place or state of oblivion. 2. An intermediate place or state. 3. A West Indian Dance done by bending backwards to pass under a successively lowered horizontal bar.

Temporary: 1. Lasting or serving for a time only, not permanent.

Transitory: 1. Lasting only a short time.

Provisional: 1. Accepted or adopted tentatively; conditional.

A PERILOUS SITUATION

The Princess did not have an assignment. She did not have a home. She did not even have a plan!

The Princess was in oblivion, the state of being forgotten. At the same time, she was well aware that the country director would not remain oblivious to her situation much longer.

The guesthouse was paid for until the end of the next week, when she should be departing for VaVa'u. It would definitely come to the CD's attention when she was still in Nuku'alofa.

Drew and the Protector each had forty volunteers reporting to them, so they had other fires to put out besides the Princess's. The Protector informed the Princess they would get together next week. Enjoy the weekend.

The group spent their last Friday evening together at the bar. During the week all the volunteers and the Tongans had jobs, and just like anywhere else, the weekends were greatly anticipated. Because of the religious restrictions in Tonga, everything had to close by midnight on Saturday. This made Friday *the* party night! And the Billfish was *the* party place.

Why? The Princess never did figure that out. The Billfish was nothing but a roof with a gravel floor, a small bar and wooden tables with plastic chairs. The menu was limited and lousy, however, the drinks were cheap. It seemed to be just another PC tradition passed on to each succeeding group. Any Friday a volunteer could show up at the Billfish and be assured of meeting up with a number of friends.

Saturday morning the Duke and the Duchess moved out of the guesthouse and into their new home. Oh, my, the Princess felt abandoned.

After their departure, the Princess walked the twenty minutes to Molisi's. Here she purchased a half kilo of minced beef (more commonly know as ground beef), a jar of tomato sauce and a box of spaghetti.

Running into the Quiet One and the Dude on her way back, she told the boys that she had enough for all, if they would care to join her in the upstairs dining area about 6:00 p.m. She was pleasantly surprised when the duo arrived with contributions. The Quiet One supplied a bottle of Australian wine; the Dude brought a loaf of garlic bread. Once again, they bemoaned the lack of an oven. The boys had become fast friends; the Quiet One had been coaching the Dude on the local vernacular. The Dude was really coming along. Unfortunately, he had an affinity for the less common aspects of the language, such as "My, you have large breasts," or "What a big butt!" The Princess had a sense of humor; she just hoped the Tongan ladies, along with their many brothers, did as well.

The boys were aware of the perilous situation the Princess was in. The Quiet One acknowledged that in his four years in Africa, it was not unheard of for a volunteer to be relocated into another assignment. He felt confident that things would work out.

During the week the Princess met with the Protector to come up with a list of possible positions. The Protector already had a plan. There was another volunteer who was currently working in a trade school. Her duties involved training young girls on sewing, cooking and picture framing. She also assisted a ladies' group with marketing their handicrafts. The school provided her housing. This volunteer wanted the available position of volunteer coordinator at the PC office. The Protector could make both girls happy!

The Princess was intoxicated with joy! Not only did she know this volunteer, she had been to her apartment. It was adorable! This was just the place for the Princess. In addition, she had the skills required for this school. Well, maybe not so much the cooking, but she was already working on improving those talents. Our Princess could sew and do needlepoint and embroidery. She could quilt, quill and make her own patterns. She was especially adept at knitting, with her forte being sweaters.

Her freshman year in high school, the Princess had started her own business. She carried her many patterns and a cardboard sign stating "Hand Knit Sweaters" to the cafeteria. Here she staked out a small table and set up shop. The student could select the design they liked, and specify colors and the proper size. For the cost of the yarn and an additional $20.00 the Princess would create an exclusive tailor-made sweater. In the first week, five days, she had ten orders! She had already made two hundred dollars!!!

In her youth and inexperience, the Princess overlooked one important detail. Knitting after school and weekends, she required two weeks to produce one sweater. You can do the math; it would take her five months to complete her orders, leaving no time for homework or social activities. Her first career endeavor failed. Nonetheless, she was positive she could handle this assignment.

At the weekly staff meeting, the Protector proposed this scenario to the CD. He was not pleased. Two others had applied for the volunteer coordinator position as well. He was not going to give the job to this girl simply to provide an alternate one for the Princess.

He was angry to discover the Protector and the Princess working behind his back. "She was brought over here for the Future Farmers, she accepted that before she came. I will not have her setting a precedent for volunteers to select and reject assignments. Send her home!"

The Protector stood her ground. "This is no longer the program the Princess signed on for. This would be the first time ever to send home a volunteer who wants to be here simply because we cannot find something else for her to do!"

Drew took sides with the Protector. "The Future Farmers is not the place for this girl. Let's give her a chance with something else."

The CD was skeptical. What job could she do? And in the meantime the PC would have to pay for her lodging. She would be doing nothing and costing money.

Ah-ha. The Protector played her trump card. She was departing for the States for four weeks; the Princess could house-sit. That would cost nothing; in addition she would have the Princess sourcing prospects for a job for herself and finalize a position when she returned.

Reluctantly, the CD agreed to a stay of execution for one month. The Princess was now out of the Future Farmers, but she quickly needed a replacement.

The Protector had a real house, a prefab three-bedroom ranch that boasted not one but two tiled bathrooms, each with a bathtub. She had a washing machine and a solar panel on the roof. There was also a TV, VCR, stereo, wall-to-wall carpeting and central air. What more could even a Princess ask for?

So the Princess was safe till the end of October, but she was fully aware that the Protector was stalling for time. The CD left Tonga permanently the second week of November.

The Commoner and the Dude left Nuku'alofa to their new locations.

The Princess moved into the Protector's great house. The Duke and the Duchess rode over on their newly purchased bikes. The Princess's bike was still boxed in storage. She was reluctant to have it put together in case she needed to take it home.

The Princess contemplated where she could be of service. She assessed her skills and past experience. How could she translate these attributes into a needed capacity that could afford to house her? All Tongan PC assignments must provide the volunteers quarters.

The Princess had rather extensive knowledge on diabetes. Her only son, the Little Prince, developed juvenile diabetes at the tender age of eight years old. Aware that fifteen percent of the population in Tonga had this disease, maybe she could be of some assistance.

She could create an education and awareness program using pamphlets, public speaking in schools or possibly providing edification on food exchanges and portion control. She took a taxi out to the hospital. It was not exactly state-of-the-art. In fact, the Princess thought that if she should get ill, she would prefer to stay wherever she was. One might die faster at the hospital. Nevertheless, the Princess needed a job. She made her way through the maze of hallways and found a nice, friendly nurse. She delivered her sales pitch. The nurse advised her they would love someone to volunteer to do something like she proposed, but they had no funds to create pamphlets, pay for things like taxis, much less to provide accommodations. Strike One.

Maybe somehow working on a recycling program—definitely a need! She made inquiries amongst the volunteers. She was told to get together with one of the guys; it was thought that he was involved with that. She approached and interrogated him. She confessed to him her problem. He informed her this was his secondary project. His initial undertaking provides his home. Strike Two.

Well, how about tourism? After all, the Princess had been a travel agent for five years. She had traveled to twenty-nine countries outside the U.S., and had taken many a tour and expedition. She had some knowledge on what people look for when traveling. Cruise ships do stop in Tonga, and maybe more would come if there were organized excursions. She could enlist some locals, or even volunteers. Why not offer a traditional kava ceremony or a class on how to weave a fan or a hat?

So, off she went to the tourist board. The Princess introduced herself to the young Tongan girl at the front desk. She inquired as to who the manager was.

"He is out of town," the girl explained, "but the assistant manager is in." She disappeared into the back rooms. Returning, she escorted the Princess to an office and introduced her to a Tongan gentleman. Again the Princess stated her case. This time it worked. This man was thrilled and would love to have a PCV. They even had a tiny house that could provide her the much-needed shelter. Great!

However, the boss would have to make the final decision. He would be in Fiji for two weeks.

The Princess was very excited. As she shook hands goodbye, she assured him she would return in two weeks.

Yippee! The Princess felt confident this would work out. Now, she could relax until the Protector's return.

She stopped by the PC office to check her mailbox. Telephones were a rare luxury in this country. Very few Tongans and no volunteers had a phone. Most businesses did have this modern convenience. The only way to get a message to someone was to physically go to his or her home or place of employment. In the case of other volunteers, the simplest way was to leave a note in their mailbox in the volunteer lounge. The Princess deposited an invitation in the compartments of the Duke, the Duchess, the Quiet One and several others to join her for dinner and game night. The only problem with this method of operation is that you can never be sure when the designated person will discover the memo.

While at the office, the Princess sat down at a table and made a long list of all the things she needed to get from Molisi's. Feeling secure that she was not going to be shanghaied on the next plane, she decided to lay in some stores for the next few weeks.

Entering the grocery store, she secured a cart, with every intention of filling it up.

Okay, let's see, what is first on the list? Dairy products.

In Tonga, the milk comes in a box and it is not refrigerated until opened. The Princess did not understand how this worked, but unopened the carton was good for six months. The same applied to juice products, like o.j.

Butter came in a block; the size was equivalent of two sticks back home. Cheese also came in block form. There was only one kind of cheese, something called "Tasty" cheese, from Australia; it was not much of a selection. There was no specification whether this cheese belonged to the cheddar, Gouda, or Swiss family, just that it is Tasty.

The frozen food section consisted of two top-open refrigerated units, mainly filled with ice cream. There were several bags of French fries; she added this product to her basket. The only frozen meat the Princess could identify was whole chicken. She selected two.

There was a fresh meat counter. This looked none-too-fresh to the Princess, for isn't meat supposed to be more a shade of red then brown? Hmm, she wondered, where does this meat originate? She had yet to see a cow in Tonga.

The bestseller appeared to be what is called mutton flaps, a four-inch slab of white fat attached to a thin, quarter-inch sliver of sheep, imported from New Zealand. She passed on the meat. As usual, later she discovered that mutton flaps are considered "unfit for human consumption" in New Zealand. They export it as pet food. The Tongans love it, because it is cheap and because of all the fat, which makes it very flavorful.

Large trays of eggs were stacked to the left of the "fresh" meat. Each cardboard container held forty eggs and these were not refrigerated. The young girl behind the counter offered her a small plastic bag; this is how one transports the delicate item home. Of the eight she purchased, two remained intact.

There were several rows of boxed and canned goods, including some vegetables, but the Princess decided she would rather go across to the Marketi to see what she could find fresh. She perused a number of other canned and boxed items. Upon discovering they were all past the expiration date, she replaced them on the shelf.

Another popular item here is *kappa pulu*. Half of an entire aisle was devoted to this product. This was the Tongan equivalent of Spam.

Dry goods like rice, flour (hand packed in clear plastic bags) and pasta were available. Paper products like plates, napkins and paper towels were outrageously priced. There was a wine section, with a choice of many varieties, all bottles imported from New Zealand or Australia. She had already learned that bottles and tin cans are very hard to dispose of. The Protector had left half a box of white wine in the refrigerator. A boxed wine was what she needed, as the packaging burns for easy disposal.

In fact, when the Princess had completed a tour of the entire shop, her list was largely unfilled. Of the items she needed, most were either not stocked or expired. This would never do. She could not make a complete meal with what she had. Making another lap, she reconsidered things she had previously passed on. This time she checked to see just how *long* they had been expired. Otherwise, her cart would have remained almost empty. It appeared that Tongans are not bothered with such trivial matters as expiration dates.

At the checkout counter, she requested they call her a taxi. She had way too much to carry on foot; in addition, her temporary housing was a good forty-minute walk.

The taxi that came for her had to be the most dilapidated vehicle on the island. The back door did not close all the way, the seat cushions were stained and torn. There was no door handle on the inside and the window would not roll up completely.

She quickly discovered that the driver was an extraordinarily sweet man. He introduced himself as John, in English, instead of the Tongan version of that name, Sione. Once he understood her desire to find boxed wine, he led her to the only liquor store in town. Here she was introduced to the smiling, heavy set Tongan lady who managed the establishment. Her boxed wine could be purchased one at a time, or in a case, consisting of six three-liter cartons. Our Princess decided this was the way to go. John carried the container to the car for her.

Arriving back at her residence, John insisted on hauling all her purchases into the house. He told the Princess that he could come here anytime she needed him. Does the Princess need to go anywhere tomorrow? He could arrange now a time to fetch her.

The Princess was not sure when she would again need his services, but "malo alpieto," or "thank you very much."

After a bit of convincing, finally he departed. Whew! He really is the nicest guy, the Princess thought, but she would actually prefer a more updated means of transportation.

That evening she managed to pull together a meal of baked chicken and mashed potatoes for her guests. She would have tried a pizza, as she figured she did have all the ingredients, but she had no knowledge of pizza dough. The Quiet One offered to put in her mailbox his copy of a paperback *Fannie Farmer Cookbook*. She looked forward to the use of this novelty.

Everyone had received their invitation and attended. Afterwards they played a game of Take Off the Princess had brought with her. In this game, the board is a map of the world, with different color routes connecting city to city and country to country. Each person has a fleet of six plastic planes; the object is to be the first to land all your aircraft on the other side of the globe. Sounds simple enough, unless another person lands on the city you are in and sends that jet back to the beginning. The Quiet One was quite competitive; he was determined to win, and he did.

Meanwhile, back in America, the presidential election was really heating up. Her father, the King, was very concerned. Daily the Princess was bombarded with e-mails, "Have you mailed your vote?" He felt especially this year each vote would count. He was prophetic, as the Duke, Duchess and Princess's home state of Florida did eventually cause much controversy down to the last vote and recount. They would never know if their votes were counted. They did not receive the absentee ballots until the third week of October. Quickly the Princess filled hers out and walked the three blocks to the post office. Even airmail to the States can take up to a month.

The Princess was enjoying the luxuries of her house-sitting, with a few minor exceptions.

A solar panel does not always ensure hot water. The definition of solar is utilizing, operated by, or depending on the sun. If there is no sun, guess what? There is no hot water.

When other volunteers requested the use of the Protector's washing machine, the Princess was firm. Washing in cold water only was permitted. Even a lukewarm shower became acceptable. Actually, it had been so long since she had had a really hot shower, she could not remember exactly what it felt like.

Another problem arose the next weekend. With the benefit of the cookbook, the Princess again entertained her friends, or at least tried to. She had two lovely pizzas prepared and ready to go into the propane oven Friday night. Everyone was there enjoying a few drinks before supper.

At the appropriate time, she unsuccessfully tried igniting the pilot light. Finally, after every male present, each one taking a turn, had attempted to instruct her on the proper procedure, even though she had performed this duty hundreds of times, it was determined she was out of gas. So, here they were a half hour from town, seven o'clock at night, with nothing to eat but two raw pizzas.

They were Peace Corps Volunteers. They were flexible. They were creative. They were adaptable. They made use of the APCD's telephone. The Princess called

John, her little taxi man, and he hurried to their rescue. How many PCVs can you fit in a rundown motorcar?

Well, at least six. Not only did he deliver them to the Friday night soiree at the Billfish, but he came back at the designated time to retrieve them.

Monday morning she again enlisted John's services. She needed propane. He took her to a gas station with an exchange program—you drop off your empty tank and accept a full replacement. This was the continuous cycle used by most Tongans. Unfortunately, this day they were out of gas! They expected a tankard in three days. Three days! The Princess had already been eating cold food since Friday night. Again John relieved her troubles. Down by the military base, on the other side of the island, was a huge propane storage facility. Within two hours, she was once again cooking with gas!

The Princess made a decision. It was time to put the bike together. It was just too far a walk from her residence to town. She enlisted a volunteer who was a bicycle maven. He made use of her tool kit, but did not require the instruction manual. He was rewarded with one of her many spare tires. She was mobile!

She visited the Duke and the Duchess. They taught at the Diploma School, in a building connected to the Tupou High School. The downtown location was known as Fasi. Tupou High had another larger location called Vaololoa, outside of town, between the Protector's house and where the Duke and the Duchess lived.

The Diploma School was the closest thing in Tonga to a college. It was very expensive, two thousand pa'anga a year. They had only twenty-six students. Two other PCVs were teachers there as well. Since the employer provides the housing for the volunteers, these four as well as another volunteer who teaches English at the Vaololoa campus were ensconced in little buildings next to each other; also included was a New Zealand volunteer.

The Duke and the Duchess shared their duplex with a female volunteer known as the Molokow Magnet, or M Squared, for short. She got this nickname because during her service she had been stung by molokows repeatedly. In the Quonset hut on the right side of the duplex lived the Kiwi, a New Zealand volunteer. Next to him was the Introvert; he was the PCV computer expert at the Diploma

School. The Artist lived across the yard behind them; he was in his late 20s. He fancied himself as quite an accomplished artist. The house next to the Artist was empty. Tongan neighbors on all sides surrounded the little group.

The Princess was envious of this little band of palanges living and working together.

One white person in a village was a standout and could be lonely. The six of them had each other for support and entertainment.

The Duchess was glad the Princess had her wheels. M Squared informed her that the downtown hotel had an in-ground pool and for three pa'anga they will let non-guests use it. So that Sunday, when everything else was closed and there was nothing to do, the Princess joined the girls for a leisurely ride and a day of suntanning.

As the girls whiled away the day, the Duchess mentioned that the Duke was on the lookout for a TV and VCR. Even though there was only one television station, there were many video rental shops. What he had found was that each piece was very expensive, which must be why so few Tongans had them. The Princess exclaimed that she had been asking around about this also and one of the other volunteers told her he had seen a great deal on a thirteen-inch combo. She was going the next day to check into it. The Duchess advised against making such a purchase immediately. She, the Princess, did not have a job yet. Not officially, the Princess answered, but the tourist board wanted her and had a house. The Protector could finalize this on her return.

So the next day, the Princess and the Duke visited the shop. The system was an American one, requiring an electric box to convert the 110 to the 220 used here. The Duke cut a deal—if they bought two they would get a discount. He also requested delivery. They agreed that the Princess would have hers delivered and stored at their house, since she had one at the Protector's house.

The next week, the Protector returned. The Princess relayed the results of her quest. Her boss was pleased. She and the Princess made a trip to the tourist board. The boss had returned. They introduced themselves and relayed the conversation the Princess had had with his subordinate. They discussed the programs, ideas, and action plans the Princess would like to offer.

This man said he was very sorry, but they were given bad information. He wanted no part of a PCV. He informed them that he had a PCV before. The tourist board had supplied his house, paid for his electricity and water, but the guy did nothing and after eight months quit and went back to America. He is definitely not interested, he said. The Protector valiantly tried to convince him that the earlier PCV was a rare exception. He wasn't buying.

This was a serious problem. The CD was on the case. With the Protector's return the Princess was back at the guesthouse, costing 10 pa'anga a day. Could the situation get any worse?

Of course it could and it did! The Princess got deathly ill. She developed a fever of 104 degrees. She shook violently with chills, yet was sweating profusely. Her throat was so swollen, she could barely swallow and every muscle in her body ached. After two days in bed at the guesthouse, she took a taxi to the PC medical office.

The PCMO bundled her into the PC van and took her to the hospital. Oh, my, the Princess was afraid this was the kiss of death. She listened as the PCMO and the doctor discussed her fate. They believed she had strep throat. They conferred on medication. The Princess requested something to make her sleep.

Then back into the van, they drove around the corner to the pharmacy. She waited in the car while the PCMO picked up her medicine. When the PCMO returned she handed the Princess two types of antibiotics and a sleeping potion. In her hand, the PCMO also had a bottle of throat spray, and she inquired if the Princess would like it.

"Absolutely," the Princess croaked.

"Well, I just wanted to make sure, as it is the last one. And I know Americans are kind of funny about expired things."

Expired or not, she wanted it. In her condition she sought any available aid. She was delivered back to the guesthouse.

Like Popeye before her, the Princess had had all she could stand and she can't stands no more. She packed a few things, leaving the rest in her tiny room. She called another taxi. Downtown she checked into the hotel, where she had air conditioning, hot water, a satellite dish with three stations, a remote control and room service.

Making use of the bedside phone, she placed a collect call to St. Louis, Missouri. Calculating the time change, it was 3:00 p.m. Friday in Tonga; therefore it should be 9 or 10:00 p.m. Thursday night in the Central time zone.

Her older brother, the doctor, answered and accepted the charges. Quickly, she described her symptoms and the prescribed treatment. Usually, he would refuse to advise treatment over the phone, but in these special circumstances he made his recommendation. She felt better already. A month later, she received an e-mail informing her that her brother had received the phone bill for her collect call. As it was $1,000, he would no longer be accepting any reverse charges. Ooooops.

By Monday, her fever had subsided and she returned to the guesthouse. By Monday, she was out of time. The CD informed the Protector, "Either she has a job by Friday or she is on the plane back to the States with me."

SALVATION

The Princess was desolate. She was crushed. She was without hope. She was out of options. How could she possibly come up with a job and a place to live in four days?

The Protector was also upset. She had vowed to save the Princess. She was determined not to let the CD send the girl home. Leaving her office Monday night, the Protector felt defeated. On her way home, she stopped by the Duke and the Duchess's house and told them what had happened.

Shaking his head, the Duke said the magic words: "It's too bad Tupou High already has so many volunteers. The principal just said to me, not two days ago, he really needs someone to fix up the administrative office. It is a shambles."

"*What*!!!" Like a phoenix the Protector rose from the ashes. "It doesn't matter how many volunteers he has, if he has a need and a house!"

Tuesday morning, the Protector was at the school. She informed the principal, Feleti Atiola, that she had a volunteer who needed a job, and that she understood that he needed help organizing the office, that using the volunteer to organize the office would help everyone. Showing him the Princesses résumé, she said, "Think about it. I'll check back with you this afternoon."

Feleti sought out the Duke. He displayed the résumé and requested the Duke look it over and advise him if this would be a match for the position. The Duke informed the principal that he was the one who suggested this person to the Protector. She would be perfect!

Three days, just 72 hours, before the Princess had passed *her* expiration date, *she had a job*!!!

Tupou High was owned and operated by the Free Wesleyan Church. Tupou High had four campuses, Vaololoa, Nukunuku, Tapunisilva and Fasi, the head office. All bookkeeping was processed through Fasi. This meant that each campus collected its own school, exam and bazaar fees and gave a receipt to the students. These fees, as well as all bills for each campus, were turned into the headquarters. Fasi deposited all the funds to the church office, requested checks for all expenses for all campuses and dispersed these checks. This office also paid all the teacher and support staff wages every two weeks. In short, all incoming and outgoing expenses were processed through Fasi.

Wednesday she was introduced to Mr. Atiola. She was taken to the office, where she made the acquaintance of the two Tongan girls she would be working with, Nisi and Sela. The girls both spoke excellent English and were delighted to have a trainer.

The small room was a mess. The carpet was ripped and torn. Boxes of old, ragged paperwork were stacked almost to the ceiling. A gigantic spider had made a home in one corner. His demise was the first task completed. The Princess noticed a large cardboard box filled with receipts and asked the girls what it was. They told her those were the petty cash receipts.

"How much do you keep in petty cash?"

"Two hundred pa'anga."

The Princess assigned herself her a second task. It didn't take a genius to figure that there were a lot more receipts there than two hundred bucks worth. It took the entire day to sort, categorize and calculate all the little slips of paper. They dated back to February, since the school year in Tonga, divided into four quarters, began on the third week of January and ended the last week of November. This appeared to be the entire year's worth of petty cash receipts. Upon questioning, the girls no longer seemed to speak much English.

Since our Princess had considerable financial control exposure, she was pretty sure she knew exactly what had happened. She added up all the school fees accepted during the year and compared that figure to the deposit book.

At the end of the day, she knocked on the door to Feleti's office, and presented him the facts: the petty cash receipts totaled 5,500 pa'anga; the deposits were short 5,300 pa'anga; they had been funding petty cash from the school fees. Feleti was extremely upset. Last year they were short a lot of money, so he had been warned to keep better control. He feared the auditor would show up any day! He decided he and the Princess would go to the church office tomorrow and tell them what had happened, but that now, with the Princess here working to organize the situation, everything would be fine.

The Protector stopped by the school to check how the first day went. Feleti told her of the Princess's dramatic discovery the first day. He was very pleased. This was the good news; the bad news was the CD. He said if she has a job, where is her domicile? He is still paying for the guesthouse, he pointed out. She needs a home, and she needs it *tomorrow!*

Feleti assured the ladies, "God will provide."

The Princess was not too happy with this plan of action. She herself had asked God to provide a number of things a number of times, with less than satisfactory results. She suspected that the roosters wouldn't be the only things keeping her awake that night.

Unbeknownst to the Princess, the Diploma School had a slightly different schedule than the high school. Her school had another two and a half weeks before the December-January break, but the Diploma School was finished the last Friday.

That very night, Feleti was driving the Kiwi, the New Zealand volunteer, to the airport, since he was returning home for the term break. On the way, the principal relayed his conundrum with the Princess.

The Kiwi offered the key to his tiny abode. "She can stay in my house while I am gone. Surely, you will have a house for her in two months."

Thursday morning, with one day, a mere twenty-four hours left, what do you know? *God did provide!*

PALANGEVILLE

The Princess moved into the Kiwi's house Friday after school. Ah, safe at last. The CD was on his way to the airport.

Plus, she was right next door to the Duke and the Duchess. It was a very small house, just two rooms—a bedroom and a kitchen with a table and four plastic chairs, plus a cement shower stall and toilet. In his shower the Kiwi had something the Princess was unfamiliar with: a solar shower. What a handy gadget that turned out to be. It was a large, heavy duty, plastic sack, with a holding capacity of three gallons of liquid and a long hose with a sprinkler head extending from the bottom. A wooden rod at the top supported the whole contraption on a strategically placed nail. With the right mixture of boiling water and tap water, one need never take a cold shower again. Of course there was no air-conditioning in the house, but she had the use of the Kiwi's electric fan. She had every window open to accept any small breeze.

Outside, to the left of the front door, was a Via Cima tank. This was a large cement cylinder about six feet high and six feet in diameter. Rainwater would run off the roofs into gutters sloping down, to be collected in the tank. Usually, one of these structures was placed about every two to three houses. Ah-ha, this was where her home-stay sister was getting that water from in the backyard. This was the water used by the Tongans for drinking, cooking and making kava. The tap water could be used for the toilet, shower and, if it is boiled, for cooking. The Princess realized that the only way for that fresh water to get from the tank to her kitchen would be for her to haul it in herself, and that going outside to fill up a pitcher would take time and be a pain. To save herself frequent trips to the tank, she purchased a five-gallon container, fewer trips. Who needs free weights?

On the right side of her was the neighborhood church. Friday evening was *the* big night at the church. First they had a few hours of singing practice.

"How lovely," thought the Princess as she unpacked her few belongings, "you don't even need a radio." She enjoyed the melodious sounds wafting across the yard while she prepared herself a meal. She was thinking how nice it was to be right next to the church.

She retrieved her new television from her neighbors and set this up on a chair in the bedroom. She popped in a video and relaxed on the double bed. As the bedroom was right smack dab next to the church, the singing was even louder. Turning up the volume to its maximum, she could almost hear the dialogue. Finally, singing practice was completed.

Then the real fun started, the *kalapu*. This was the casual form of the kava party. It was a guy thing; the only female present was one they paid to be the to'a. Every Friday night at almost every church, town hall or school assembly room, there would be a kalapu. All the men would get together, sitting around a rectangle on straw mats, smoking and drinking kava. The kalapu would last all night long, beginning around 8:00 p.m. and lasting until three or four in the morning.

Well, at least they were not too noisy. The Princess turned out her light and retired for the night. She was awakened in the wee hours by the sound of someone retching right outside her bedroom window. No sooner did this guy complete his business than another joined him! Oh my God, they are so full of kava they cannot hold any more. They vomited to make room to return to the party. Our Princess was beginning to rethink how nice it was to be right next to the church. She closed the window, preferring the warmth to the special sound effects.

Over the weekend she got together with her neighbors. The Duke and the Duchess had a very large patio. M Squared and the Introvert joined the threesome, and the Quiet One stopped by to see how things were going. They chatted, played cards and decided to pool their resources for dinner.

Early Sunday morning the Princess was jolted out of her bed! The church bell, that resounds village wide, now was clanging *right* outside her window! Oh, it was deafening! That cinches it, she thought, I am positive it is not so nice to be right next to the church.

There was another problem. The pigs! The house of the principal of the Vaololoa campus, Mapele, was in front of their houses. For some reason, he had a huge pigpen between the duplex and the Artist's house instead of in his own backyard. The pigs were constantly getting out. They were very destructive, digging up the yard, wallowing and defecating everywhere.

The Duke and the Duchess were adamant that they would not tolerate this. Within minutes of a pig escaping, one of them was at Mapele's door complaining. The Princess was in agreement with them, but as she was only a temporary resident, she was reluctant to complain too much. The trio had no idea what a constant battle this would become over the next two years.

Another problem was garbage. The only was to get rid of it was to burn it. Previous tenants had apparently burned their trash willy-nilly anywhere in the yard. There were a number of black patches all over the place. The Duke obtained a cylinder of sheet metal. He located it as centrally as possible to the volunteers and they unanimously used only this round container for trash burning, letting grass re-grow elsewhere. The Duchess planted small trees and flowers. The palanges were fixing the place up.

Despite the difficulties, the Princess very much enjoyed living in "Palangeville." Each night she had the option of being alone in her dwelling or seeking out the companionship of the other volunteers. They borrowed the proverbial cup of sugar and exchanged paperbacks. Most evenings they shared something for dinner and discussed the day's events, even if just for an hour.

In addition, of the forty volunteers on the island, they were the only ones who had televisions, so they became quite popular. There was only one television station in Tonga and the broadcasts were sporadic. There was no TV guide, so you never knew what you would find on. In addition, programming didn't operate on the hour or half-hour schedule used in the States. It might be twelve minutes or twenty minutes after the hour when programming changed. Sometimes you would receive a video of local singing, sort of an MTV Tongan-style.

If any show involved a kiss, the programming was interrupted with dolphins leaping in the ocean for thirty seconds, returning to the show after the kiss had been blacked out. Every once in a while, a movie was shown. The Princess called out her window to inform the Duke that *Lawrence of Arabia* was on. He answered her call, "What channel?" To their dismay only the second half of the classic was shown.

Within a two-mile radius of Palangeville were four video rental shops. These were all little mom-and-pop operations. The films were home-recorded elsewhere and shipped to Tonga. If you were lucky, you got the entire movie. Many times the tape stopped before the movie did. You also could get a written message on your screen: if you had rented this it was against the law; this tape was the property of such-and-such studio.

Though his house was in the yard behind the Duke and the Duchess, they rarely saw the Artist. He kept to himself and he taught at another campus, so they didn't see him at school either.

The Quiet One still did not have a village to go to. He was now staying at the PC headquarters in an apartment above the medical building, and several other male volunteers were ensconced there as well. He came out frequently to visit Palangeville. One evening he stopped by to tell the Princess a secret.

"I know that the Artist is going to ET," he revealed. This was PC lingo for early terminate or, more plainly, he was going to quit. "You should ask Feleti for his house right away, before someone else does."

"But I haven't seen it. Have you? Is it nice?" she asked.

"Nice! Well, that's relative, isn't it, but it's twice the size of this place. With a little work it could be fixed up."

The Princess had a new mission: get permanent residence in Palangeville

Permanent: 1. Intended to serve or function for a long or indefinite period.

Stable: 1. Firmly established, enduring. 2. Not likely to give way.

Habitable: 1. Capable of being inhabited.

Address: 1. The place where a person or organization is located. 2. The location and name of an intended recipient indicated on a piece of mail. 3. A formal speech.

Domicile: 1. A permanent legal residence.

TUPOU HIGH SCHOOL

The curriculum at the Fasi campus was Forms 4, 5 and 6, which is the equivalent of our high school. There were approximately 250 students. All lower grades were at the Vaololoa campus.

A long rectangular building housed the administration office and four classrooms. At one end of this structure sat the assembly hall, with the library upstairs. Across the backyard were two more buildings with classrooms. To the right of the main building was the Diploma School.

The receipts that were given for all fees were in bound books of three hundred. During that particular year about twenty such books had been used.

A gentleman stopped by to pay the balance of his child's annual dues. He wanted to know what he had paid so far. Nisi and Sela divided the books between them and started to go through page by page, looking for this child's name throughout the entire year.

The Princess discussed this with the principal. "We must have a computer," she said. "We could set up now before the next year, all students by name and form. Any time they make a payment we will enter that amount and receipt number. We can know at any time how much has been paid and what is owed—not just per student but for the entire school."

Feleti agreed with the Princess and the next day she received an elderly computer.

At the end of each day all monies collected were locked in the safe. The Princess started the girls on a schedule; deposits were taken to the church office three times a week.

Meanwhile, the Princess became familiar with all the staff at the school. The teachers were friendly and welcoming to her. She feared she would be disliked because of all the rules she was putting in place. Instead, she found everyone liked the organization and structure she was providing.

One of the most interesting things the Princess discovered was that when you meet a Tongan, the first thing they would ask about would be your family. "Are your parents still alive? How many brothers and sisters do you have? Are you married? Do you have children?"

When you meet someone in America the first question they usually ask would be, "What do you do for a living?" There is no translation in Tongan for the word *career*.

The school fees generated all income. This amount was slightly over two hundred pa'anga a year per student. A discount was given for each consecutive child in a family. In Tonga, large families were the custom. In fact, if you had less than four, it was common knowledge there was some kind of a problem. The average family had seven children.

The money coming into the school was never enough. They could not even afford workbooks; Xerox copies of entire text were the norm. Chalk, pencils, rulers and especially staplers were difficult to keep hold of. The Princess learned quickly never to lay down her pen. Another lesson she learned was that there is no theft in Tonga. Something may be "borrowed" but never "stolen." Dozens of ballpoint pens, a number of plastic rulers, and two staplers were "borrowed" from her.

She gradually became aware and was amazed that there was no school lunch program or cafeteria, not just here but throughout the entire island. It appeared they were unfamiliar with the American custom of "brown bagging." The children had nothing to eat from 8:00 a.m. until they went home at 4:00 p.m.

She and the principal discussed the possibility of opening a snack shop for the students. There was a small building being used for storage. Feleti agreed to have it cleaned out and made available for the Princess. She would come up with a plan of operation by the beginning of the new school year, next January.

One afternoon, when Feleti was thanking the Princess for her assistance, she saw her opening. She still needed a house; they could not wait until the Kiwi returned before they addressed the situation. He advised her that the Protector had made him aware that another of his volunteers might be leaving. She had heard this as well, and she wanted that house. The principal suggested she get the key directly from the boy, so as soon as he left she could move in.

Meanwhile, a number of the staff came to the Princess to complain that they never got their wages on time. Currently, they were ten days past due. How can that be, wondered our girl. She sat Nisi and Sela down and they informed her, it was true the wages were always late. The church office told them that Tupou High didn't have enough money deposited to cover this amount.

The Princess realized the school was operating close to the bone; nonetheless the staff must be paid. She made a trip to the church office, sat down with an officer and was educated. The wage requests from Tupou High were never turned in on time; also, the calculation was always inaccurate, which explained the continual delay.

Returning to the office, she coached Sela on the beauty of Excel spreadsheets. They would create a page for each campus, with staff members arranged alphabetically, and deliver the spreadsheets to the church office seven days before wages were due.

Another discovery regarded the bank loans—the local banks were reluctant to make loans to the Tongans as they constantly defaulted. Who could blame them when the average wages translated to eighty-four U.S. dollars a month? The banks would make loans to the school staff with a letter stating they were employed, then the school would deduct the funds from the person's pay. The loans were repaid directly by the school.

The Princess made a promise: not once in the rest of her time in Tonga would anyone receive wages late. As we all know, a Princess always keeps her word. Not that this was an easy covenant to maintain.

Every two weeks, she updated the forms, added and subtracted loans, wrote the check request and delivered the documents to the office.

As the employees were all paid in cash, she had to write out each name and amount on a little envelope; she had to do this for ninety people. Upon receiving the check, she made a trip to the bank, requesting the total broken down into the correct number of 20s, 10s, 5s, 1s, 50 senitis, 20 senitis, 10 senitis and 5 senitis. She and Sela would count out each amount and seal in the pouch. If they made a mistake and had money left over or not enough, they would have to open up each pouch and start again. All three banks loans had to be paid that day. At the school, everyone's favorite day was payday—everyone except the Princess.

HOME AT LAST

School closed for the break. The Artist left early December and the Princess got the key to her permanent home. Before she could move in some restoration was needed.

The Artist did not have the same tastes as a Princess. He had aqua walls with bright orange stars spaced around and had empty tin cans nailed to the ceiling molding around the entire kitchen. There was ripped linoleum in one room only; the rest was bare cement floor. The furniture was sparse. In the living room, there was a single wooden slatted bed with a foam cushion; this was pushed against the wall and used as a couch. The kitchen held a wooden table with two plastic chairs. In the bedroom were a two-drawer chest and a cabinet with a wooden dowel, as there are no closets in Tonga houses.

All her neighbors helped her paint, wash the glass louvers and lay new linoleum. It was three days before she could move in.

As an extra bonus feature, the Artist left her his dog! The Princess wondered how in the world she was going to get rid of that snaggly toothed, mangy mutt. He never left a five-foot perimeter of the house. As she had no dog food, she fed him whatever she ate—chicken, bacon, mashed potatoes with gravy.

Bibi became her devoted slave in no time. One afternoon, she heard the dog barking furiously on the front porch. Stepping outside, she saw a big Tongan guy in the bright yellow and blue uniform of the Tonga Electric Power Board outside of her fence. He requested she hold her dog so that he could come over. What did he want? Why, he wanted to disconnect her electricity, the bill was overdue. She told him she had just moved in two days ago, that was not her bill. This did not satisfy the fellow, but any time he attempted to cross over the fence, Bibi lunged at him. The Princess assured him that she would clear up the matter in the morning. Having no choice, the electric man left. Bibi was removed from his limbo status and was granted permanent residence.

With time off from her job, the Princess set about making her house a home. She had curtains made for all the windows. She purchased four plastic chairs and a double bed with a mattress. She hung the mosquito net provided by PC over the bed and received her PC stove/oven and the little refrigerator. Since this fridge was so tiny, the size of one found in dormitories, she also purchased a full-sized one.

Each month, she received a care package from her parents. Along with her cigarettes, she received a solar shower and packaged food products that were not available in Tonga, such as Cheetos, Stove Top stuffing, chocolate chips and *People* magazines. Since there are no bookstores in Tonga, the magazines were especially valuable. The volunteers all swapped books, and a small exchange library had been set up in the PCV lounge.

The Princess was a little afraid in her new house. Since she was across the yard from the others, she was worried that if something happened in the middle of night no one would hear her if she yelled. With her new, constant companion Bibi, she knew she need not fear. The dog seemed to have a sixth sense as to who was friend and who was foe. Any volunteers or Tongans from school that stopped by were never accosted, while others were not allowed over the fence. Bibi received a flea collar and a rawhide bone in the next package from the States.

Then the Princess had an epiphany. There are six volunteers living here together. Why not pool their resources and purchase a washing machine!

She shared her idea with the others and they readily agreed. The Duke scouted out the available product; there was not much to choose from. The Duke discovered several used machines but as far as new, they had a choice of only two models, since not many Tongans owned appliances. The statistics they received stated that in Tonga about one household in one thousand had a washing machine, one in five hundred an oven, and one in one hundred a television. The Duke collected the money from each volunteer; they covered the Kiwi's portion until he returned. The washing machine was delivered. They installed it on the front porch of the duplex right between the Duke, the Duchess and M Squared. Needless to say, only cold water washing was available.

In doing laundry at home, the pigs were a constant source of irritation. Hanging clothes out to dry, one found oneself standing in pig manure, which came with swarms of flies.

One afternoon the Duchess went out to check the status of her laundry, to discover two wild dogs having a tug of war with her bath towel. They had brought down the entire line—all her clean clothes were lying in the pig poop! When the Princess heard shouting in the yard she looked out her bedroom window to see the Duchess fighting the dogs for her towel. Fearing she would be attacked, the Princess grabbed a broom and charged out of her door. By the time she rounded the corner of her house, Bibi was nipping at the heels of the mongrels as he chased them over the fence.

The Duchess had had enough. She rode her bike to the police station. What is the law, she wanted to know, about unpenned pigs. She was informed that by law, pigs were required to be penned, but no one did. When she pressed as to what recourse was available to her, she was told you could shoot any pig that was in your yard.

Armed with this information, she pounded on Mapele's front door. She asked to borrow his shotgun. He informed her that he did not own a gun and wondered what she needed one for.

"I just came from the police, and they told me I can legally kill any pig in my yard. I will not live with pigs! I will kill them with my machete if I have to!"

For several months after that, the pigs were retained in their pens.

The Protector stopped by one day and told the Princess that a temporary CD was arriving for three months. The Protector knew him from previous Peace Corps service. They had worked together in PC Thailand. Great, the Princess planned a dinner party.

The Princess held her dinner party. She served fried rice and a spicy Korean snapper. The Protector brought the new CD; the Duchess, the Duke and M Squared also attended. What a change from his predecessor. This man was delightful. He was open to problems facing the volunteers, what projects they were working on, and he was caring and compassionate.

During dinner a large pig was rooting along the outside of her fence when suddenly he broke through to the inside yard. The Princess jokingly said to the dog, "Bibi, get that pig out of my yard." He leapt off the front porch and chased that pig right back out the way he came in. Everyone was very impressed. Bibi's star just kept rising.

The Princess never learned why, but for some reason the local children had a toy that was only brought out during the Christmas holidays. A six-foot bamboo pole was hollowed out. A little spout was inserted near one end. They poured kerosene into the pole and blew into the spout again and again, building up some pressure. Then they threw a lit match into the pole, causing a small explosion. They would sit outside and do this for hours. It was quite annoying.

Christmas also meant that the Little Prince was coming to visit. The Princess couldn't be happier. He arrived on Wednesday; his luggage did not accompany him. Fortunately, he had all his diabetic supplies in his backpack. The Duke and the Quiet One loaned him clothes for the four days it took for his gear to make an appearance.

After the thirty-six hour trip from Atlanta to Tonga, her son was exhausted. Unfortunately, a nap was out of the question because of the continual bombs exploding outside. That night he passed out early, on the couch, and the Princess retired to the bedroom. About 4:00 a.m., she was awakened. The Little Prince had pulled open the mosquito netting and was shaking her.

"Mom, wake up! Mom, someone is being attacked! Right outside the window."

The Princess sat up in bed "What? What's the matter?"

The Little Prince was insistent. "Don't you hear that?"

She listened, and then laughed. "Oh, no, that's just the roosters. You'll get used to it," she replied before she rolled over to go back to sleep. She heard the Little Prince muttering to himself. "Roosters. I thought roosters crowed at dawn."

That Friday night they all took him to the Billfish. They walked out to the main road to hail a taxi. The Princess advised him to pay attention to where he was and the route they were taking. The Little Prince would probably stay out later than she would want to.

"Okay, what is the address?"

The *address*? This sent them all into fits of laughter, as only the few main roads had street signs. Nothing else was named, much less had a number applied to it.

At the bar they ran into the Dude, who was over from Ha'apai for the holidays. He assured the Princess he would look out for the twenty-year old.

The Princess arrived at her home about midnight. She noticed that Bibi did not greet her.

She was tired and a little tipsy. She went straight to bed.

In the morning she prepared French toast and bacon for her son and her dog. She called out the door, but Bibi did not appear. Now, this was very strange. She got dressed and went around Palangeville. He was nowhere to be found. She was concerned but didn't know what else she could do.

For several days there was no sign of her dog. In the month since she had moved in, Bibi had never once left the yard. Spotting one of her Tongan neighbors, she asked if she had seen her dog. The lady responded she didn't know she had gotten a dog. Why, she had adopted the dog the Artist had left. Oh, *that* dog! The woman seemed a little upset.

The Princess felt this person was withholding information. She persisted in her queries.

Reluctantly, the news was divulged. Some naughty boys had thought the dog was abandoned. They had taken him. Okay, where did they take him, for she wanted him back. Oh no, that would not be possible, those naughty boys, they *umu*ed him.

Oh my God! They *ate* her dog! The Princess was distraught. She was disturbed. She was angry. All the wild dogs roaming this island and they chose hers to eat! The Duke suggested she didn't do him any favors by fattening him up.

The Princess decided the Little Prince needed to help out with the chores. She asked the Little Prince to burn the trash. He looked in the bag she handed him.

Little Prince: "There is Styrofoam and tin foil in here."

Princess: "Right, so you have to get the fire good and hot for the foil to melt."

Little Prince: "So, you burn anything, even though it is toxic?"

Princess: "How else do you think we are going to get rid of it?"

Little Prince: "Oh, I don't know, maybe a *recycling* program."

Princess: "Gee, why didn't I think of that?"

There was not much in the way of entertainment in Tonga and the Little Prince was accustomed to the booming metropolis of Atlanta. The Princess enlisted others to help keep her son occupied. The Duke took him on an hour-long bike ride to the village of Kolivi, home of the famous fruit bats. There were hundreds of them, hanging upside down in the trees. At maturity these bats have a three-meter wingspan. This is rather impressive.

The Dude took him kayaking out in the ocean. They spent the entire day paddling out to Pongi Motu and back. The Little Prince got sun poisoning. His feet and ankles were seriously swollen.

The Quiet One, who had finally gotten a home, took him out to his village for a kalapu.

The Princess suggested he ride around to the video stores, and gave him all her membership cards. The Little Prince had worked for Blockbuster Video for three years after school. Upon his return, he exclaimed, "You call that a video store? They have no categories, they have everything all mixed, and they don't even have a list of the inventory!"

Somehow the boy still managed to find five movies to rent. When the Princess commented on the number, he said, "We got nothing *but* time here, Mom," relaxing on the couch with his first installment. The Princess laughed to herself, waiting for his reaction when he was minus an ending of a movie.

The Princess decided to have a New Year's Eve party. She invited the volunteers left on the island. This was about twenty, since a large group had gone together to New Zealand and the rest back to the States. The Duchess assisted her in making five lasagnas. They needed every person in Palangeville to cook one in their PC oven, commonly referred to as the "easy bake oven," based on its size and the fact it had two temperatures, High and Super High.

The Little Prince had brought his mother another game, Cranium. This board game is a combination of Trivial Pursuit and Pictionary, and incorporates spelling words backwards and humming a tune for your partner to recognize. It is played in teams and was a huge hit. Everyone enjoyed it. They drank, ate and partied till midnight.

Then the younger volunteers came up with a brainstorm. They would all ride to the wharf and jump into the Pacific Ocean to celebrate the New Year.

The Princess wanted no part of this. She understood the Little Prince wanting to go along, but was afraid he would never make it home. A married couple that lived not too far from her assured her they would see he got home. So they all hopped on bikes and took off, leaving the *elderly* to tidy up the place.

The Princess had trouble going to sleep, as she was worried about the Little Prince. About 3:00 a.m. it started raining; actually, it was more like a monsoon. Now she was really worried. He showed up an hour later, dragging the bike behind him. He had wiped out in the rain and in the morning he would need to make use of the tool kit.

The Princess asked, "So, everyone went swimming in their clothes?"

Little Prince: "No, we jumped in *commando style*."

The Princess had a pretty good idea what this meant, but decided not to verify.

Odyssey: 1. An epic poem attributed to Homer. 2. Any long adventurous journey.

Journey: 1. Traveling from one place to another taking a long time. 2. To make a journey.

Adventure: 1. An exciting and unusual experience. 2. An uncertain and risky undertaking. 3. To risk or hazard.

Peregrinate: 1. To travel or journey, especially on foot.

2001: A TONGAN ODYSSEY

The second week of January, with the departure of the Little Prince and her dog, the Princess was sad. She decided to get started on her second project at the school, opening the Canteen.

She sat down and created a business plan, dividing her opening stock into classifications: beverages, sandwiches, ice cream, and a variety of chips, candies, lollipops, chewing gum, noodles, dried fruits, and school supplies.

She discovered that Coca-Cola had a small distribution center in Tonga. She made an appointment with the manager, placed an order and secured a small cooler to keep the drinks cold.

She found two other vendors that carried enough variety to supply the main products. She also discovered a bakery that would deliver cream buns, fish burgers, cinnamon buns and loaves of fresh bread daily. She planned on making their own sandwiches, egg, tuna, and—she was the first to introduce this classic to Tonga—the peanut-butter-and-jelly sandwich.

She created Excel spreadsheets to track her inventory weekly. The principal promised he would deliver her an employee on the first day of school. With one week to wait, she was prepared and ready to open.

Meanwhile, back in Palangeville, with the absence of Bibi, there were several strange occurrences. In the middle of the night, once again she was roused from her sleep. What she heard sounded like someone whispering, very faintly, then a louder, rustle, rustle, rustle noise followed by a thump. This occurred a number of nights in a row. She was too frightened to get up and investigate.

The next Friday evening, several volunteers were over watching a movie in the front of the house. When the Princess used the bathroom in the back of the house, she could hear this noise through the window. Rushing back into the TV room, she murmured to the Quiet One. He quickly snuck outside; a few minutes later, he could be heard speaking in Tongan.

When he returned, he had solved the mystery. Some young boys were stealing the breadfruit from the tree right outside the Princess's bedroom window. They would whisper to each other, and throw rocks to knock the breadfruit down, which caused the thumping sound. He instructed the boys they could have all the breadfruit they wanted, but they must come in the daytime because they frightened her in the middle of the night.

Sunday is an incredibly long and boring day in Tonga. With nothing open, and no work permitted, including laundry, it seemed endless. There was no television and of the two radio stations the one that broadcast Sundays was all religious music. Of course, there was a choice of three church services to attend, but as these were completely in the Tongan language, the Princess only attended on special occasions.

Everyone seemed to enjoy the Cranium game so much that the Princess started a tradition of her own. Every Sunday around three o'clock, any volunteers within biking or walking distance were invited to her house. Everyone must bring some food for potluck. After the several hours it took to play the game, they all cooked up dinner. They soon got organized and had a weekly theme, such as Italian or Mexican. The boys contributed a few pa'anga instead of bringing food. Soon Sunday became the day to look forward to instead of dread.

The end of January, Tupou High was again open for business and so was the Princess. She spent mornings in the Canteen with her newest employee, Sita. The afternoons she was in the administration office.

Sita quickly was at ease and enjoyed her new position. She felt like she was running her own small business. She was honest and hardworking. The bakery delivered daily, and the other vendors once a week.

This was really working out. They operated on a very short margin but they had the advantage of not having to pay rent, electricity or wages. After replenishing the merchandise, they started socking some money away in their own little bank account.

The Princess had the bright idea that if they had a stove, sink and refrigerator they could cook something hot each day for the students and make even more money. M Squared gave her the idea to write a Small Project Assistance Grant to submit to the Peace Corps. Each quarter a committee reviewed all SPA Grants and voted on which ones to fund.

The Princess enlisted the Duke to help her. Together they created a work of art, though if the truth were told, it was mostly the Duke's doing. The Princess described exactly what she had in mind, and then he presented this in the best light in the official SPA format. The plan was that at the end of each term the Canteen would donate to the School all the proceeds after restocking.

After they submitted the document to the Peace Corps, they had to wait to see if it would get approved.

The Princess noticed that the school fees the Vaololoa campus was delivering to the girls to be deposited were less than Fasi's amounts. Finding this very strange, she approached Feleti, who confirmed that Vaololoa had more than twice the number of students, approximately six hundred. They must not be enforcing that the fees be paid. When the principal contacted Mapele (the principle of the Vaololoa Campus), he was adamant they had collected over twenty thousand pa'anga and delivered this to Fasi.

"Well, then we really have a problem," she declared. "Our records indicate a little over twelve thousand."

It was obvious: there was a thief amongst them. Feleti questioned the girls individually. They denied any knowledge of this problem. The church office was notified since this was a *lot* of money in Tonga. They sent an external auditor, and he and Feleti repeatedly interrogated the girls.

Finally, one cracked. She confessed. This was a huge scandal in the school. My, my, the teachers shook their heads and thought how sad it was she needed the money so badly. She was relocated to a department where she would not have access to funds. In addition, from this day forward, Vaololoa's fees would be collected directly at Fasi.

Now the Princess had the additional burden of creating spreadsheets for the six hundred students at Vaololoa, and collecting all the fees, *and* with one less person in the office.

The Princess was astounded. The money had been spent, and it could not possibly be repaid. Since the girl only made 160 pa'anga a month, how long would that take? Plus the girl did not even get fired. She wondered what the motivation was for anyone here *not* to steal.

She soon discovered the power of shame. Within a month, the youth was gone, banished to an outer island. This is the Tongan way. Actually, the Princess preferred this action versus sending her to the one prison. This offered the girl a fresh start.

Each morning before school, there was a morning assembly, finishing with the children singing. Singing is the most important social event in Tonga. Twice a year, there is a singing competition, and every school in the country enters.

Many times formal classes are cancelled in favor of singing practice. At first, the Princess personally believed that science, math, and history should be more important than singing. Even so, the sounds of the children's voices, a cappella, was so beautiful that a number of times she was brought to tears listening from her little office. Over time she came to realize that the Tongan culture did not revolve around math, science or history, but around family, religion and interdependence upon each other. Three percent of the population in Tonga was over sixty. Life was hard. Life was not long. Each family grew almost all of their own food, tending to the crops and gardens after completing a full day of work. Fresh water was hauled into the house, and the laundry for a family of ten was washed weekly in a plastic bucket. Most Tongans slept on a straw mat on the cement floor. A dozen people would live in a five-room house. Singing for them was a source of pride and self-esteem.

Unfortunately, the song "Who Let the Dogs Out" found its way to the Tongan airways.

It was an instant hit. It could be heard wafting from cars, drifting down hallways and floating on every breeze. Our Princess had no doubt that for the rest of her life, that song would always carry her back to Tonga.

That weekend the Princess and the Duchess rode to the wharf, locked up the bikes and took the tiny boat the half-hour to Pongi Motu.

Ah, there they found the lovely sandy beach they had imagined. It was very pristine, with a few plastic lounge chairs, and not crowded—only two dozen people were there that day. It was also very hot, so the girls got in the water to cool off. They were able to wade out quite far in the outgoing tide.

Wow, look at that! There at her feet lay beautiful, bright, royal blue starfish. They entranced the Princess; she had never seen anything like it. The Princess was still watching the starfish when she noticed the Duchess had returned to shore.

Then she noticed something else she had never seen before. A movement caught her eye. Inches from her swam the dreaded black and white *banded snake*.

Wow, look at *that*! They had been informed about this during training. If you get bitten by the *banded snake*, don't worry. It will kill you in exactly seven seconds! There was no antidote; there was no time for one. Well, our Princess was not born in a manger but she certainly was walking on water that day in her haste to return to land. Never again in the next nineteen months she spent in Tonga did she stick so much as a big toe anywhere other than the swimming pool at the hotel.

Soon the Princess was notified that she was receiving the grant money. They made plans to remodel over the next term break. During the waiting period, she realized several other things she should have included in the budget. She would like to build a covered seating area for the children, which would cost approximately another seven hundred pa'anga.

The Kiwi was returning to New Zealand permanently. Unlike the Peace Corps volunteers, the school had to provide the oven and refrigerator for the Australians and New Zealanders. They also paid them wages. When the Princess noticed the refrigerator being picked up from the Kiwi's house, she got an idea. If they could put that in the Canteen, that would free up just about enough money for the patio. The principal agreed with her. When she was ready, she could have the fridge for the Canteen.

Meanwhile, without her watchdog, the Princess returned home one day to find her electricity had been disconnected. The next day she complained to Feleti and it was reconnected. The next month her electricity was again disconnected as well as the Introvert's and M Squared's.

This time the Princess asked her remaining girl, "What is the process of paying the electric bills?"

She learned that they wait for all bills to be delivered from all the campuses and from teacher and volunteer housing. Since all the meters get read at different times, the bills are late. The electricity gets disconnected all the time. The Princess had a problem with this. Further questioning produced a list of forty accounts. The Princess brought this to Feleti's attention. They both believed this was a lot of accounts, even for four campuses. The principal sent a young fellow around to put a name to each account. Only about fifteen were not the school's accounts. The Princess put a list in the computer with a name assigned to each number. She took this to the Tonga Electric Power Board and requested that all the bills be delivered together to Fasi once a month. This solved the problem.

Late February, a signup sheet was posted in the PC lounge. This was a notice that a new group was arriving, so a head count was needed for the bus going to the airport to greet them. When a current volunteer noticed the Princess did not put her name on the list, he questioned her. This is a school night for the Princess, she replied, and she had no intention of staying up till two in the morning. Besides, she can see them plenty over the next year and a half.

PCV: "Right, but you only have twenty-four hours to place your bet."

Princess: "What bet?"

PCV: "All the current volunteers have the first twenty-four hours to place their bet on who in the new group will be the first to quit."

Princess: "How rude! How barbaric! Hey, wait a minute. Did you do this with our group?"

PCV: "Are you kidding? With your group we had to change the rules."

Princess: "What rules?"

PCV: "Everyone has to choose a different person. Since everyone chose you, we had to add a time line. Giving you three weeks or two months, like that."

Princess: "Well, I am still here!"

PCV: "So, nobody won. It happens."

It was almost time for the next term break, when they could remodel the Canteen. Going over her spreadsheets, the Princess noticed they were not depositing as much money as they had been. She walked across the schoolyard to discuss this with Sita. Entering the Canteen, she saw Sita bent over writing in a notebook. Peeking over her shoulder, the Princess gasped!

The girl stood up and hid the notebook behind her back. The Princess held out her hand and demanded, "What is that?"

Sita blushed crimson. "Nothing."

Our Princess knew exactly what it was. She pulled the paperwork from the girl's hands and waved it in her face. "This is *credit*! There is no credit here. I told you that on the first day. Why? Why? Why would you do this?"

Sita started to cry. "Because they ask me, because it is the Tongan way."

Fuming, the Princess stormed across the campus into Feleti's office. She would not have this! There would be no credit. She had established this before she opened the Canteen. Everyone at the school had been doing this behind her back!

It was clear to the Princess that the principal was not aware credit was being accepted at the Canteen. It was also clear that he did not see the problem with credit.

Again she tried to explain that since they were operating on such a tiny mark-up, they could not offer credit. Besides that, credit in Tongan translates to *free*, since no one every pays it back! They would be completely out of business in a month.

She was fighting a century-old battle. The Tongans share everything with everyone. This was why it was very rare to find any Tongan in business for himself. If they opened a shop, then the aunt, cousin, sister, brother, any relative would stop by and, according to tradition, the business owner must share. Obviously, after giving away all of the inventory, they would fail.

The Princess refused to budge on this issue. She understood it was a cultural thing. She knew they could not fathom why she had a problem with it. However, she had worked too hard to pull this little cigar box operation together. She told the principal that she would not accept the money for the SPA grant from PC. This would be deceitful; she had turned in a business plan that did not reflect credit. She would no longer have anything to do with the Canteen.

Well, there is one thing a Tongan will never do. Let free money slip away! The next day, at morning assembly, the principal announced there would be no credit at the Canteen; in addition, he gave the list of credit owed to the head teachers. Anyone who did not pay this money back would not be permitted to purchase anything at the Canteen.

Foolishly the Princess believed she had heard the last of the credit issue.

During this school break the Canteen was remodeled. Cement was poured for the seating area for the students, with a sheet metal roof. Formica was glued to the plywood worktables. A sink and some storage cabinets were added, as well as a propane stove and oven. Pots, pans and cooking utensils were purchased. She just needed to locate the stored refrigerator. This proved a difficult feat. No one seemed to have any knowledge of it.

Finally, she sought out the principal. Oh, yes, the refrigerator. Yes, he had promised the Princess that item. He would go and tell his wife to clean it out. It seems his old refrigerator had broken down, and since he did not have the money to replace it, he had been using the Kiwi's.

Oh my! The Princess could not take the refrigerator and leave this man and seven children without. At the same time, she could not operate without one. What is a Princess to do? She went shopping for the least expensive one she could find. She had no choice but to pay for it herself.

Of the new recruits that had arrived and were now in training, one would be sent to live in Palangeville after the swearing in. For his Peace Corps assignment, he would be an industrial arts teacher at Vaololoa; he was known as the IA. An Australian teacher had already replaced the Kiwi. This meant, once again, another house was needed. The handyman at the school was sent to fix up the empty house next to the Princess's.

In March, the Duke and the Duchess had moved across the yard into the newly decorated dwelling. The Quiet One had come out to assist the Duke with heavy items.

While they were hauling all the belongings from one place to the other, the Princess had made peanut butter cookies. The boys were inside reconnecting the "easy bake oven" and the Duchess was outside chatting with a Tongan neighbor who had stopped by. The Princess had a platter of warm cookies for the two men;

she knew both had a sweet tooth. Before entering the front door she paused and offered the treat to the Tongan neighbor. This lady was all smiles, as she made a pouch out of her skirt and tipped the entire batch into it. "Malo, Malo alpeito," she called as she hurried off.

The Princess and the Duchess exchanged a glance over the now empty dish. The Duke, who had witnessed the incident from inside, called out the window, "Were those *my* cookies?"

They all laughed at what slow learners they were, and the Quiet One explained. Any time something is offered in Tonga, this means the person doing the offering is finished. Now, he tells them!

While the girls had repeatedly behaved in the American custom of offering one or two of an item, the Tongans were responding with their custom of taking all home to share with their families. The Princess had made five dozen, though, so there were more than enough.

The two buildings were spaced about eight feet apart. The *pssst* of a soda can opening could be heard. When one household operated an electrical appliance, the other lost TV reception. They could converse through the open windows.

That evening, the Princess heard shouting coming from next door. The Duchess flew out the screen door, over the fence and out into the dirt road. Before the Princess could put down what she was doing to investigate, the Duke came outside as well, carrying an orange hose. He and the Duchess both entered the Princess's front room.

The Duke had been reading while the Duchess went about preparing dinner. She lit a burner and within minutes flames were shooting out from behind the stove. The rubber tubing that connected the propane tank to the stove was on fire, and burning towards the tank.

The Duchess shouted a warning to her husband and fled. The Duke took a risk and stayed to turn off the flow of gas. This extinguished the blaze. They could have been killed! A propane tank exploding might have taken out half the neighborhood.

The cause of this arose when the men had moved the equipment and reattached the hose—they should have placed it along the bottom of the floor; instead, they ran it up against the back of the wall, where it was exposed to the heat, causing it to catch fire. The first meal in the new house was cooked at the Princess's.

The Duchess set about starting a large garden. She enlisted several local boys to help her hoe, till and plant. They chose an area in the backyard between this house and the duplex. Corrugated sheet metal was installed as a fence. She planted tomatoes, lettuce, corn, radishes, peppers, basil, dill and parsley.

Right outside her family room window, facing the Princess's house, the Duchess spent several days installing a variety of green plants and flowers. Each afternoon she hauled buckets of water to nourish them and seemed tireless in her efforts to keep weeds out.

Break was over, and it was back to school for the Princess. The new and improved Canteen reopened. Each day of the week, along with the sandwiches and bakery goods, the Princess cooked something hot. Monday was pizza, Tuesday was sloppy joes (her mother had sent her fifty of the seasoning packets), Wednesday was some form of pasta and Thursday, fried rice. As Fridays were always a half-day and the children left at one, she didn't cook.

Business was good. There was one problem: any food that was left over at the end of the day needed to be disposed of. The Princess felt the only thing to do was throw this away. Which she did. And this created the problem.

In a country this poor, no food was ever thrown out. The Tongans thought she had gone completely insane! They wanted to take any excess home. She tried to explain that if they did that, no one would buy anything, but would wait for the freebies at the end of the day. The Princess realized nothing she could say would make this acceptable. You might recommend that the excess be delivered to a homeless shelter, but there are no homeless in Tonga. So the Princess did two things: first she lowered the number of each item, hopefully to sell out. Second, she herself purchased whatever was left, took it home and threw it away there.

The new volunteer moved into the half of the duplex that the Duke and Duchess had vacated.

The Princess usually arose at 7:30 in the morning. She had stopped attending the morning assembly, since it was all in Tongan and she didn't absorb much of it. She would depart for school about 8:45. About a month after the Duke and the Duchess had moved in, the Princess was getting ready for school when she happened to glance out her window.

Oh no! She saw the pigs were out and were trouncing the Duchess's beautiful flowerbed! No sooner did she notice the destruction than her neighbor's screen door banged open. The Duchess flew out of the house in her little shorty pajamas and her sneakers. She hopped on her bike and took off!

The Princess was amazed at this sight and she stepped out on her front porch. Now the Duke was outside as well. He was throwing rocks to chase the pigs away. She asked where had the Duchess gone. Well, you could have knocked our girl over with a feather. The Duchess had ridden up to the Vaololoa campus to storm into the morning assembly, in front of the teachers, Mapele and six hundred kids, to demand that something be done about the pigs this instant! In her shorty pajamas! Sometimes a girl's gotta do what a girl's gotta do!

She did get quite a reaction! Within the hour the pigs were once again behind bars.

Though the volunteers hoped they'd see less of the pigs, they were sad that the time had come for them to see no more of the Protector. Each PC assignment is two years, for volunteers, the APCD, and the CD. Sadly, the Protector's tour had ended. A group of volunteers took her for a last dinner at the Sea View. This is *the* fine dining in Tonga. The husband of the couple that owns this place is the chef, and his wife is the business manager and hostess. It was truly delicious. They had several bottles of wine and a sad goodbye.

♛

Meanwhile, back on campus, the credit issue once again reared its ugly head. During a staff meeting the teachers suggested to the Princess if they could have credit at the Canteen they would purchase more. Very diplomatically, she had to admit that she was sure they *would* purchase more if they had credit, since they would never pay it back! Obviously, they were in cahoots! They had a brilliant idea: she could collect what they owed every two weeks from their wages. They could not imagine why this was not a great idea. Again the Princess explained, *no credit*, the Canteen did not have enough mark-up to only collect money every two weeks, as she would not have enough to keep stocked. In addition, once credit was started it would quickly get out of control—next the students would want credit and they had no way to get money from them! Lastly, she felt it would be to easy for the staff to run up a large bill in two weeks, and then the wages they received would not cover more important bills. There was to be *no credit*!

♛

Stopping by the Peace Corps office to check her mail, whom did she meet but the Dude? Oh my God! The boy had lost so much weight. He acknowledged he had lost about forty pounds. He had been having quite a few problems in Hai'pai. He was very unhappy. In fact, he has just ETed. He would be flying home the next day.

Oh no! The Princess asked if he and his buddy the Quiet One would like to come over, and she would cook up something special. She was very sorry to see him depart.

♛

Once again in Palangeville, they had a big pig problem. There was a large spotted pig that somehow kept getting in the yard. Every inch of the perimeter had been inspected. There were no holes in the fence; there was no loose area to crawl under. The Duke, M Squared and the Princess were discussing this matter when the Duchess came down the dirt path on her bike.

The Duke told her that the spotted pig was inside the fence again. They could not figure out how he kept getting in.

"I know," the Duchess calmly stated. "He jumps over the fence."

Even her husband had to try not to laugh at this ridiculous idea.

"A pig is not built like a dog," he told his wife. "A pig cannot jump over a two-and-a-half foot fence."

The Duchess was indignant that they didn't believe her. She took her bike and huffed off.

Several days later the Princess was outside burning her trash. Uh-oh, she spied that big spotted pig on the other side of the fence. Grabbing a rock, she started towards him. When, what did her wondering eyes behold? That big pig reared back on his haunches and *jumped* over the fence! There he stood, big as life in their perimeter! M Squared exploded out of her door. "*Did you see that?*"

They chased the pig, and he turned around and, neat as you please, he sailed back over the fence the other way! No sooner did the porker take off around the corner than the Duke came riding up. When he saw the girls he wanted to know if they had seen how the pig got out.

They looked at each other and burst out laughing. "You'll never believe it."

This pig could not be kept out. He had to be sent out to a village where no palanges threatened his life.

The biggest challenge that faced our Princess during her two years in Tonga was the *critters*.

Let's begin with the ants. Whenever it rained, which was often, the ants moved inside, creating their own highway system that would rival any in Los Angeles.

After dousing them with Moritein (the local pesticide), she had to sweep aside the thousands of bodies.

Moving on to the roaches: these were not usually seen in daylight. At night, lying in bed with the mosquito net firmly tucked under the mattress, she heard them. The roaches threw more parties in her kitchen than the Princess did.

Then there were the geckos. They also shared her kitchen. They scampered up and down the walls, playing hide and seek with each other behind her calendar and photos. The only real problem with the geckos was that they left tiny bits of excrement behind them.

She considered them a sort of pet that didn't require feeding. At least she didn't think they required feeding. One afternoon she made butterscotch pudding. Setting this on the counter to cool before placing in the fridge, she completed her other chores. Returning to the kitchen, she picked up one of the containers—imagine her surprise when out of the center of the pudding burst a gecko. He balanced on the side of the glass for a split second before leaping to the counter and scampering away.

The molokows were a cause for great alarm. Remember, they grow up to six to eight inches and inject poison with their fangs. They come through the smallest crack; they climb straight up the furniture or walls. They attempt to crawl across the ceiling, till gravity pulls them down. This is why so many volunteers are stung in bed. This is why the Princess used a mosquito net. This is why she purchased a metal bed frame—they cannot climb up a slick surface. They can even enter the house through the pipes. Nothing can stop your heart like leaning over the sink to brush your teeth, and having one of these things pop out. They hide in the doorframes, and when you open the door they fall down on your head. Everyone fears the molokow. The molokow is capable of bringing even the strongest of men down.

Lastly, but in the Princess case, most importantly, was the spider! The spider in Tonga is as large as an adult's outstretched hand. Huge! They can show up anywhere, in the kitchen, in the bedroom, even while you are sitting on your tuffet in the bathroom. These are no ordinary spiders—besides the size, these spiders play dead! They would curl their eight long legs underneath them, not moving, fooling the Princess into leaving them alone until she could get a neighbor to remove the body…later to find no dead body, and wondering, where he is hiding now. The spider caused the Princess the heebie-jeebies the duration of her stay.

Since the Princess was from Florida, the country's hurricanes were not a new experience for her. The really bad weather started on a Monday afternoon. Heavy rains, thunder, lightning caused by a hurricane; the storm was reported to be stationary out in the ocean. The tin roofs echoed the noise throughout the house.

Tuesday morning the school lost all power and the children were sent home. The Princess went across the yard to help close up the Canteen. Instantly her umbrella was turned inside out and she was soaked to the bone. Her long, culturally sensitive skirt clung to her legs; her hair was plastered to her head and the straw kia-kia around her waist smelled like a bale of wet hay. Seeking shelter under the awning, she found the noise from the vibrating sheet metal to be deafening. Just then the bakery showed up with her delivery. Oh no! She should have called to cancel.

After battening down the hatches of her little shop, she was blown back toward the office. She was wading in flip-flops through calf-high water with God-knows-what floating in it. She shared a taxi home with the Duke and the Duchess. They were barricaded in the houses for seven days. Power was out for many hours, long enough for the food in the freezer to thaw, causing internal flooding to add to the external flooding. The louvered windows had to remain closed to keep the rain out, which made it very hot. School was canceled for the week. The airport was closed; the only runway was under water. The Princess wondered to herself, the Peace Corps! What could I possibly have been thinking?

The following Tuesday, the rains stopped. The sky was a brilliant blue and there was a slight breeze in the air. When the Princess arrived at school, the students welcomed her by name. Several teachers were waiting for her. One had a list of English vocabulary words she needed explained. Another wanted help writing a letter in English. A third asked for help with trivia questions for the quiz club. Ah, the Princess thought, the Peace Corps. This is what I was thinking!

Walking over to the PC office to check her mail, the Princess ran into one of the Tongan staff. With her was an American lady, the replacement for the Protector. The new APCD and the Princess became great friends during the time they were in Tonga together.

Another quarter of school was over. At the last staff meeting the Princess made a presentation. The Canteen had a profit of one thousand pa'anga to give to the principal and personnel. It was completely up to them to decide what to do with the money. They were very excited. Should they choose new uniforms for the rugby team, repair the broken toilets in the bathrooms or maybe fix up the teachers lounge?

The Princess and another volunteer took a trip to Samoa for the vacation. The flight was brief and inexpensive. Wandering around downtown, they made their way to the PC Samoa office. There were several volunteers in the lounge. That very night one of the volunteers was holding a huge party for all the others on the island. They were invited. The assignment of this country seemed to be quite different than Tonga. These volunteers had cell phones! They had garbage pickup! They had a McDonald's! The Princess very much enjoyed her stay at the world famous Aggie Grey's Hotel. She even got a massage!

The Princess returned home July third. Many of her friends had e-mailed her from the States, "Do you have the 4th of July in Tonga?" The reply was, of course, it comes right after the third of July. Do Tongans celebrate American Independence Day? No.

It just so happens that the King Taufa'ahau Tupou IV was born on the 4th of July, so this date is a national holiday, with banners and lighted signs all over the island. Everyone is welcome to participate in the annual parade with a float. In Tonga this means a flatbed truck with people waving from the back.

The new permanent country director had arrived and was throwing a barbecue at his house. Grilled chicken and pork were provided along with beer and wine. Everyone was asked to bring a dish. The Princess made a cheesecake, potato salad and peanut butter cookies. A volleyball game started off the afternoon, with a boom box and dancing winding up the evening.

Once again she marveled at the change in the replacement from her original country director. This man was just as charming as he could be. Over time the Princess grew not only to respect her CD but to enjoy him as a friend. It must have been some strange fluke the first one was so awful.

With the success of the Canteen at Fasi, the Princess decided the larger campus of Vaololoa needed one as well. After all, they had a lot more students. She didn't think her chances of getting another SPA grant so soon were good. The eighty volunteers serving in this country could all turn in needed requests. The committee rotated their selection. There was only so much money to go around. It would not be fair for one person to continually get funded.

This time there was not an existing building to modify. This time they would have to build from the ground up; she would need twice as much money. Instead of applying for the grant, she decided to raise funds a different way. Her approach was to create a brochure, with photographs of the children, the school and the Fasi Canteen on the outside. On the inside was her plea for donations. This was e-mailed to Kinko's in Florida, where two hundred of the tri-fold were printed. Her father picked them up and her mother mailed them to anyone and everyone they had ever known. The Princess waited to see who would contribute to a need in a country most had never heard of.

At one of her Sunday afternoon parties, a volunteer asked if everyone had heard about the men who had escaped from the prison. The two had been convicted of rape and incarcerated. Somehow they had broken out. From the looks of the enclosure, this didn't appear very difficult—it looked more like a farm than a penitentiary. A large area of land on the far side of the island was enclosed by a five-foot-high wire fence. The convicts spent their days planting, growing and harvesting crops, providing not only their sustenance but also a small income to cover expenses of their confinement.

Anyway, true or not, as the story went, the bad guys busted out, and hid right in this village, in a house just around the corner, right across from the video store. They were at a cousin's place. This was big news; all the neighbors were talking about it. There are no secrets in Tonga. The police were not concerned. Where could these two go? If they had any money, the only option was to an outer island. They didn't have a passport to leave the country. Within a few days word got around to the authorities and they went to the "hideout" and picked them up. There were no repercussions on the relatives for "aiding and abetting."

"So," the Princess asked, "they are back in jail?"

"Actually, now they are dead. At least, that is what I heard—they both hung themselves in their cells," responded the PCV. Everyone thought that was rather strange. Somehow they both managed to hang themselves right after returning to the lockup.

Another volunteer offered an opinion. "All in all, Tonga is a pretty safe country to be stationed in."

The party conversation amongst the volunteers evolved into a discussion of when a crime is not a crime. A crime is an action that is legally prohibited, they reasoned. Small rules like not penning pigs is technically a law, but not enforced. Who would do the enforcing? Everyone is related, and no one would be imprisoned over the pig issue. Therefore Tonga *is* almost totally crime free. Rape and murder are the only real actions against the law.

There is no theft in Tonga. Theft is the act of stealing. For example, let's say that Viliami finds his car is not where he left it. He reports this to the police. This is a small island, and within three or four days the police will find the car parked at the home of Tevita.

They knock and say, "Tevitia, isn't that Viliami's car?"

He responds, "Yes, I needed to borrow it for a few days but I am finished now. Thank him very much."

The car is returned, case closed. In Tonga, everyone maintains there was always the *intent* of return. In the case of money, they keep maintaining this until everyone forgets about it. To borrow is not a crime. The father of the girl who confessed to taking the school fees continuously promised to pay back the funds, although as far as the Princess knew, not one seneti was ever seen.

There is no crime of wife-beating in Tonga. A black eye, a swollen lip or the occasional broken limb is not spousal abuse. Every man in this country will tell you: sometimes you must remind the little woman of her place. This was common and accepted. This was not a crime. One of the volunteers said, "At one time this was also common in our own country. A well-kept secret."

There is no crime of child abuse in Tonga. The Princess herself witnessed what she was afraid would be fatal blows. Yet the children were respectful and mannered, and contributed without complaint to the daily chores. Another volunteer burst out, "Even a five-year old will learn this lesson to not be beaten!" To which another responded, "Well, there is no alcohol or drug abuse; there is no casual sex. It would be rare indeed to find a pregnant teenager." Every child needs discipline. This is not a crime.

This is a religious country. The Holy Bible is full of tales of chastisement and reprimand. Why, it is common knowledge in Tonga that any ailment or serious illness is God punishing you for not enough prayer or poor church attendance. Yet another volunteer piped up, "Some missionary really sold these people a bill of goods. When Captain Cook arrived they were still cannibals."

Uh-oh. Several volunteers were getting rather animated. This was changing from an interesting discussion to a rousing argument. "What works here works," the Quiet One suggested. "This is a tiny country with few inhabitants. Imagine if the two to three hundred million people in America could all 'borrow' from each other." Ah, a little levity quickly diffused the situation, to the Princess's relief.

The principal of Tupou High, his wife and seven children lived on campus. Their house was behind the Diploma School. Needing the key to the safe, the Princess went looking for Feleti at his home.

Making a list in her mind of a number of deeds she needed to accomplish that day, she was lost in thought, and almost tripped over a large horse lying on its side right outside Feleti's door! Oh my God, how did *that* get here? She was astonished. Not only was this the first horse she had seen in Tonga, it appeared to be quite *dead*.

The principal emerged from his door. "Yes, did you need me?" He spoke casually, as if it is perfectly natural for a dead horse to be in the front yard.

After securing the key she came for, curiosity got the better of her; she had to ask, "Why is there a dead horse here?"

The answer was simple enough; he has to supply the meat for a wedding feast this weekend. The Princess was quite glad she would not be attending that ceremony.

Monday, four days before wages were due, one of her favorite teachers had a problem. Last month he had requested she stop subtracting the loan from his pay. Thinking his loan had been repaid, she complied. Now he wanted her to reinstate the deduction. She was very sorry, she said, but the wages were turned into the church office last week. He would have to wait until the next pay period.

He was extremely distraught; sweat broke out on his forehead. He insisted that would be too late. She encouraged him to share his problem with her, that whatever it was, it could not be that bad. This twenty-eight-year old was the oldest son. When his father died he took over as head of the family. The loan he was paying was the mortgage on the family house. He had stopped the payments last month because he needed the money to pay for his sister's wedding. His understanding from the bank was that only two payments could be missed. He must pay this week or he would be in default.

The Princess found this hard to believe, but to ease his mind she offered a suggestion. She knew another PCV whose assignment was at the bank. She would call her friend and find out what is what. Check back with her after lunch.

The Princess called the other volunteer and relayed the information, including name and account number. Several hours later she received a call back. Yes, missing the third payment would result in foreclosure. Oh, come on, for the equivalent of 130 U.S. dollars they would take his house? How could this be? The PCV had a solution: "I assumed you would vouch for this guy, so I went to bat for him. He has been granted an extension until the next pay period, then he pays double, 180 pa'anga, and he will be back to only two delinquent payments. That is acceptable."

The Princess really appreciated all the effort put forth by her fellow volunteer and thanked her profusely.

When her teacher returned, anxious to hear what she'd found out, she told him the good news. He was sorry he caused her so much trouble, but that would not help. Tears came to his eyes. He cannot pay double. It was a hardship as it was with the ninety, leaving only thirty-five pa'anga for each two-week span. He just did not have ninety extra pa'anga in his pay.

Oh, for heavens sake! If he pays the ninety she will loan him the other ninety, she told him, and take five pa'anga every two weeks till he pays it back. Ninety pa'anga to her was forty-five dollars; she did not want this on her conscience. There was one stipulation: he could tell no one! She was already owed twenty pa'anga from two other teachers and fifty from another one; she was not the Bank of America.

One afternoon, the Quiet One stopped by as he had noticed she had a package at the office and brought it to her. She invited him to stay for dinner. She had been waiting for this package. Her solar shower was tattered and torn. The rubber had a gash near the top extending from one side almost completely across. It was barely hanging on. She had requested another be sent.

She unpacked all her goodies and laid the new solar shower over the towel bar outside the cement stall. She would have to climb on a chair to remove the old one and it still had some water in it. She wondered how she would get rid of it.

Her friend suggested it would burn; after all, it was just rubber. In fact, while she prepared dinner he offered to burn all her trash, including the now obsolete shower. With the meal on the table, he called to her. "Hey come look, I told you it would melt." They both stood and watched as the plastic shrived into nothingness.

The next morning the Princess arose and enjoyed her usual Diet Coke and smokes. Then with the kettle boiling she stepped on the chair to retrieve her new solar shower. At first, her mind could not grasp why the new arrival had a rip, side to side, exactly like her old one. Then her sleepy faculties wrapped around the truth. Oh my God! Last night they had stood there and burnt the *new one*!

Once again in the middle of the night the Princess's sleep was disturbed. She heard a rustle, rustle, rustle noise and a thump. Believing it was the boys back for breadfruit, she got up and peeped out into the darkness. There was no one behind her house, but someone was behind the Duchess's house and appeared to be throwing something into a tree there. The tree was not a breadfruit tree, and it was over behind the other house. She went back to bed.

In the morning she questioned the Duchess. "Someone woke me up again in the middle of the night. They were right behind your house. Did they wake you?"

"That *was* me! There was a big rooster in that tree crowing right in our bedroom window, and I was throwing rocks to try and roust him."

That evening the Princess heard shouting coming from the house next door. She looked out the window in time to see, once again, the Duchess hop on her bike and ride off! When the Duke came onto the patio she also went outside. "What's going on?"

The Duke was taking a shower when he noticed a horrendous smell. Rushing to the kitchen, thinking the oven was again on fire, he found the Duchess boiling a pot of rice filled with *Crystal Drano*! Inhaling the fumes is hazardous. He threw the concoction out the back door, pot and all, yelling at the Duchess in the process. He thought he hurt her feelings. Why, the Princess wanted to know, was she making Drano rice? The Duchess had believed that rice was something a chicken or rooster could not resist. They would eat the poison-infused rice and die, allowing her the ability to get a peaceful night of sleep.

It was hard to believe how quickly the time was passing. It was anniversary time, one year since Group 59 had been sworn in. The Princess planned a small celebration for the four. Even though it would be a Tuesday night, she invited the other three over for dinner.

Monday she was planning her menu for the next day's party, thinking it would be fun to repeat the first meal they had prepared together, of macaroni and cheese—with the help of Fannie Farmer, she had perfected this dish, in fact, as the saying goes, she had "kicked it up a notch" with the addition of baked ham and broccoli. Now, they could toast garlic bread. She had her shopping list completed, when there was a knock on her screen door.

The Quiet One was in town and he didn't want to make the hour bus ride back to his village tonight, only to make the return trip tomorrow for the anniversary party, could he crash at her place? Of course, she welcomed him in. After dinner the Princess retired, while her companion watched videos late into the night.

SEPTEMBER 11, 2001

Before time for the Princess to arise, she heard someone run between the two houses and pound on the Duke and the Duchess's door. She could hear the Duke talking but she could not understand what was being said. Minutes later, another person ran between the houses and joined the conversation. This was M Squared.

Inside her house she heard the Quiet One using the bathroom. He stopped outside her room and inquired, "What is everyone doing running around so early? It is not even seven o'clock."

Just then, they heard the Duke shouting, calling their names. "Wake up! Get up! Turn on your TV. *America is being attacked!*"

The Princess could not rip the mosquito net away and get out of the bed fast enough! The Quiet One already had the one station tuned in. Fox News was on!

Then, the most unbelievable sight imaginable was replayed again and again: two separate planes smashing into the Twin Towers of the World Trade Center. It was surreal. It could not be true. This was followed by the destruction at the Pentagon. Lastly, the final plane was downed in Pennsylvania.

Tuesday morning, Sept 12, at 7:00 a.m. in Tonga was 2:00 p.m. EST in America, September 11, 2001.

The six volunteers in the two houses were struck dumb. They watched the horrible tragedy that had unfolded as they slept last night. How can people be so cruel to each other? What a world we live in.

Two hours later, the four that were teachers got on their bikes and left for the campus. They still had classrooms of students waiting for them. The Princess and the Quiet One remained glued to the set. Around ten o'clock the Princess took a shower and dressed. She left the Quiet One at her house and set off for the school.

Upon arrival, several teachers were in the office. They stopped talking when she came in. Her Tongan friends were so sorry to hear what had happened in her country. They wondered how much of her family had been killed? The Princess burst into tears. Everyone came to her side and put their arms around to comfort her.

They had no understanding of exactly what had happened. How could they? The tallest building in Tonga is four stories tall. If you took every man, woman and child on this island, that might equal the number of people in those two towers. They could not believe she did not personally know every one of the people killed or injured, as in their country, where even the latest newborn is known to all. They could not fathom why you would need a building that tall, what it could possibly look like in real life, or why that many people would be in such a building. It seemed to them like a big budget blockbuster movie with great special effects.

Once she started she could not stop crying. She went to the principal's office to notify him she could not work today. He was very understanding; he had been to America, so he understood more than most Tongans. He volunteered to drive her home. No, she wanted to walk over to the Peace Corps office.

Entering the volunteer's lounge, she encountered a group of her peers. They were transfixed to the news. All the girls were sobbing uncontrollably, the boys were angry.

They should ET right now and hunt down the dirty dogs that did this and wipe them off the face of the earth. This scenario was not helping our girl. She went to seek out more rational heads. The APCD was in her office, composing a letter for everyone's mailbox. Since most volunteers do not have television and the radio broadcast mostly in Tongan, the PC needed to get reliable, responsible information to the volunteers. The ones on the outer islands might not even be aware of the situation.

The Princess spoke of what she heard downstairs. The APCD assured her that no one would be allowed to ET in this state of mind. Everyone needed to calm down. The best thing would be for them to keep working, to keep the mind busy. The Princess understood, and she would return to her post tomorrow. She needed today to grieve.

In Palangeville, the Duke was back, only having one class that day. He and the Quiet One were together at his house. She joined them; they could not tear themselves away from the broadcast. They still could not quite believe they even were receiving live news from the States. There was no celebration that night, they did find solace in numbers and all were together.

Fox News continued for several weeks. E-mails from the States requesting her return were followed with news of anthrax and high terrorist alert status. At the moment the Princess felt safer in Tonga than anywhere in else in the world. Most people have never heard of it, and if by some chance they have, they don't know *where* it is.

The one television station in Tonga resumed regular broadcasting. The volunteers were without current updates except through e-mails and information on the Internet. Tonga returned to normal.

For months after September 11th, no mail was received from America. She had rationed and spaced out her cigarettes as long as she could, but they were not endless. She ran out.

Each day, thinking surely by now, some mail has gotten through, she walked to the PC, checked her mailbox, then the mailroom, thinking maybe the packages had not been sorted. Nothing. She made her way the three blocks to the post office, checking in the back where she knew the packages were delivered from the airport. Each day the results were the same. After two weeks of this, the Tongan lady at the post office said to her, "It hurts my heart to see you come every day and nothing for you. There are only two planes a week from America. No need to come every day."

Oh, okay. The Princess got the feeling she was being a nuisance to this nice lady. The next day she did not go to the post office. She simply returned home after school. Later, while the Duke was outside hanging up his laundry, she heard him say, "Yes, she lives right here, in this house." Curious, the Princess stepped outside, where a Tongan lady was calling to her from her car.

Not recognizing this person, the Princess walked up to the vehicle. Why, it was the post office lady! She informed the Princess that she has packages, that two had just arrived for her. Hop in!

The Good Samaritan drove her to the post office, let her get her packages and returned her to her house.

"However did you find me?" the Princess inquired?

Well, everyone knew the Princess worked at Tupou High. The lady called the school and was told she lived in Palangeville, so she came looking for her, knowing she had been waiting for her packages. How could a stranger be so nice to her? What a world we live in.

Time: 1. The duration of all existence, past, present and future. 2. A system of measuring the passage of time. 3. A limited or particular period or interval.

Construct: 1. To build by putting together parts. 2. Something constructed.

Headwind: 1. A wind opposed to the course of a thing.

Poison: 1. A substance that has the inherent tendency to destroy life. 2. To put poison into or upon.

LIFE GOES ON

The total amount collected for the Vaololoa Canteen was slightly over eleven thousand pa'anga. The money was wired to the Princess. She decided to hold a meeting with the parties involved on the placement, size and construction of the building. She knew that the issue of credit had to be firmly addressed. She refused to resume the daily struggle she had faced in the past on this issue.

All the Tongans agreed to assemble at 5:00 p.m. in the teachers' lounge. The Princess was the first to arrive at 4:45. She had her notes in order, ready to chair the gathering. When she was still alone at 5:30 p.m., she realized she forgot to make allowances for *Tongan time*.

This is far different from American time. In America, time is money, we have places to go and people to see, appointments and schedules to keep. In Tonga, nothing is urgent, there is nothing that cannot be done tomorrow instead of today. Still alone at 6:30, she gave up and rode her bike home.

Annoyed that no one showed up, she ate a light meal and watched television. Hearing a knock on her screen door, she was surprised to find three of the Tongan staff on the porch. They wanted to know why the Princess was not at the school. Didn't she request a meeting on the new Canteen?

Checking her plastic watch she responded, "Yes, at *5:00*. It is now *8:30!*"

The teachers gave her a bewildered look. "So, we are all there now."

She was irritated. She was absolutely not returning to school at this late hour to begin a lengthy discussion. It would have to be rescheduled. Good night!

In the morning, she discovered the teachers found it odd she did not attend her own meeting. She suggested they get together that afternoon at two, knowing full well they would all be in class at this hour. They all agreed, with no remark from anyone about the conflict.

Again she arrived at 4:45; several teachers had preceded her. By 5:00 everyone was in attendance. Ha, there is more than one way to skin a cat!

Placement was decided, and that the male students would complete construction. The Princess wanted to find someone she could really trust to be the construction supervisor, as this person would have access to the money. She decided to approach the IA, the industrial arts teacher.

The Princess invited her neighbor volunteer over for dinner. She discussed the entire project with him, and wanted to know what he thought. He relayed to the Princess his situation.

He was brought here with the assignment to work in a vocational school. He was informed this would be for older boys, who had already graduated. This school would be teaching a craft, working to develop skills in plumbing, electrical and construction skills. At sixty years of age, he was not happy dealing with immature children just making plywood coffee tables.

Not only could the Princess put herself in his shoes, she had already walked in those shoes. She could empathize completely, that the project originally accepted turned out to be something quite different. She explained to him that it was a dream of Feleti's to build a vocational school and he requested volunteers from PC for that end. The request was sent to Washington and the job filled by the IA. Feleti made plans and assumed everything would fall into place, that God would provide. Unfortunately, in this case the dream was unfulfilled, which is how the IA ended up doing what he was doing.

The IA told the Princess he would be delighted to organize and oversee the construction of her Canteen. It would get him and the students out of the classroom. Instead of coffee tables, the boys could really accomplish something. However, he would needs blueprints, actual working plans. He asked if the Princess knew the PCV working at the Tapunisiliva campus, since that girl's degree was in architecture.

Once again the Princess was amazed at the power of Peace Corps: each volunteer with a different skill, all working together to put in a piece of the puzzle to create the whole. What would she have done without the help of her peers? Through them she had received help with computer programming, the SPA grant, bank loans, design and construction of the Canteen and, in times of stress and emotion, a shoulder to lean on.

They had to go back to the drawing board twice. When the first completed plans were priced out, the project was too expensive. They downsized the entire structure and connected it to the assembly hall, eliminating a wall. On the second try they got it right. Construction on the Vaololoa Canteen began in November, three weeks before the term break.

Late one afternoon, the Princess and the Duchess were departing Fasi at the same time. They set out on the bikes single file towards home. For most volunteers, island transportation is a bicycle. And there is a strange phenomenon in Tonga: it does not matter which direction you point your bicycle, you will, without fail, be riding into a strong headwind. The good thing is that the land is completely flat. The bad thing is the packs of wild dogs. You need not pay attention to the vehicles on the road, for they will go around you, but at all times keep your eyes peeled for any sign of a dog. You have no idea how fast you can peddle when you hear the unmistakable snarling of a pack of mongrels behind you. Like the wind!

On this ride, the Duchess wanted to stop for a loaf of bread. The bakery was a mere ten-minute ride from Palangeville. The Princess was in front of the Duchess, cruising along at a nice pace, when suddenly, out of nowhere, they were assaulted! From behind, the Princess could hear the snapping, growling menaces closing in for the kill!

Our Princess was a few years younger than the Duchess, but nowhere near as athletic. She heard a shriek from her friend behind. Knowing the limits of her bike-riding abilities, she dared not turn around. If she did, her hands would steer the handlebars the way her head moves. She would end up as dog food in a ditch.

She called out to the Duchess. Hearing the return shout, "I'm all right! Keep going!" she picked up the pace. Her legs became a blur pumping around and around the small circle that powers the bike. When they reached the turnoff from the main road to their dirt path, they stopped. Attempting a sharp right at that speed would result in a wipeout. They had outrun them!

The Princess was worried. "Did you get bit, is that why you yelled?"

The Duchess was furious! "No, they were nipping at my heels. I threw the bread at them and they stopped."

The Princess thought to herself, that might not have been a good idea. Now, every time the dogs see them they might think they would get fed.

The Duchess had had enough! No one does anything about these dogs! Not the Tongans! Not the Peace Corps! She is going to take matters into her own hands!

Friday night, the Quiet One stopped by on his way to the Billfish. The Princess preferred to stay home, but offered up a glass of chilled white wine. The two were relaxing in the TV room when they heard a screen door slam. They had a perfect view of the Duchess standing on her front porch. What was she doing? What did she have in her arms? It looked like a big platter of something. It looked like…could it be…meatballs?

The Duchess glanced around the yard. She called out, "Here doggie, doggie…." Then she whistled…*whet, whet, whet*. She called out louder, "*Here, doggie, doggie….*" She whistled again…*whet, whet, whet*.

Oh my God! The Princess and her friend were hysterical. She was calling the wild dogs. After the Drano rice, the Princess knew what the Duchess had in mind: Drano meatballs.

The two were falling off their chairs laughing: these are wild animals—they don't come when called.

Hey, look at that! One raggedy dog slunk over the fence. Soon, another and another appeared. When she had six mangy mutts at her feet, the Duchess started throwing them the raw meat. At first they shied away, used to having rocks thrown at them. Quickly they figured out this was food. Then they figured out, the woman was the source. They went after her! The Duchess flung the tray at them and escaped inside the house.

The dogs devoured all the meatballs and sat there waiting for more.

"Great," the Quiet One called out the window. "Now, we are trapped inside."

"Ha, ha," calls back the Duchess. "They will all be dead in the morning!"

In the morning the Princess had her usual Diet Coke and smokes, then showered and left for work. She had forgotten about the previous night's event—until that evening, around the same time, out her window, appeared first one and then another and another *dog*!

Not only did the poison not kill them, now they showed up nightly to be fed. It was two weeks before they either forgot or figured out that no more meatballs would be offered.

When the Princess is wrong she admits she is wrong. She had to admit; she had misjudged the Commoner. She had not seen this volunteer in a long time when she came upon her in the PC lounge. The Commoner had toughed it out up in the Niuas for fifteen months, living in a thatched hut with no running water or electricity.

She had been successful in organizing the growing and grinding of kava to be shipped to other islands, providing a small income for her youth group. The poor thing was having medical problems. She had developed a serious rash all over her body, including her face, leaving pockmarks. So far, none of the treatments had had any effect. The rash was creating permanent scars. She was brought to the main island for the PCMO to see the problem firsthand.

Another year had passed and once again, Christmas was coming. The Princess was going to meet the Little Prince for two glorious weeks in Australia. How exciting. The Duke and the Duchess were going back to the States for a few weeks.

Dining together before departure, the Duchess had a bright idea. She planned to bring back enough electric fencing to enclose the compound. This would solve all their problems. The dogs, the chickens, the roosters and the pigs, she can electrocute them all!

This was news to the Duke. He asked his wife if she had taken leave of her senses.

"First of all," he asked, "do you know how much that would cost? Second, how do you propose to plug it in? Thirdly, most importantly, it would not only take care of the pigs, chickens, roosters and pigs, but any small child that happened along!"

That was the end of the electric fence idea.

The Princess met the Little Prince in Sydney. They spent a week touring that beautiful city. Bondi Beach, the Aquarium, the Opera House, the Little Prince even climbed the Harbor Bridge. They flew out to Alice Springs for New Years Eve, and the Princess had booked a trip to Ayres Rock.

What she thought she booked and what she booked turned out to be two entirely different things. The brochure read, "Early morning pickup from your hotel; four-hour motor coach drive to Kings Canyon, to view the beautiful vistas and amazing rock formations; then a stop for lunch before arriving at Ayres Rock for sunset viewing, followed with an overnight at a permanent campsite." The photos in the brochure showed people snapping pictures of the beautiful vistas and amazing rock formations and four people peeking out of a tent on metal bunk beds.

They *were* picked up early from the hotel. They *did* drive for hours on the motor coach. However, when they reached Kings Canyon, which the Princess thought was going to be nothing but a Kodak moment, they pulled into a large empty parking lot. The tour guide pointed to a huge plateau, straight up on both sides and flat on top. "Okay, this is Kings Canyon. What we do is start here and climb up this side, then across the top, then down *into* the Canyon and back up the other side, ending with coming down Cardiac Hill. This will take about three and a half hours. Bring your water bottles.

"Oh, by the way, remember in Australia all the snakes and spiders are poisonous, so keep a lookout. Let's go."

Oh my God! This was not what the Princess had had in mind at all. A three-hour *hike*! Cardiac Hill! Poisonous snakes and spiders! The Little Prince was thrilled, running ahead to take the point up the side of the mountain. The Princess asked the tour guide if she could wait in the bus. No way, everyone has all their possessions in there, he couldn't leave anyone on the bus.

She had two choices: sit in the parking lot by herself or go along. She went.

The Princess started out in the middle of the pack, but quickly was bringing up the rear. Don't forget, our Princess was a smoker. By the time she reached the top of the mountain her heart was about to pound out of her chest; she was breathing in huge gulps of air, like someone on oxygen, which she could have used a little of at that point. Collapsing on the first rock she came to, the Little Prince came over to her. "Mom, did you check that rock for snakes and spiders?"

The Princess leapt into the air. "See, you're not as tired as you thought."

The Princess noticed the Little Prince had finished all his water in the first hour. She chastised him. He should have been rationing the water to last the entire time.

"Oh please, that is for old people. Besides, I am fully hydrated now."

Guess what? Within another half hour came the plea. "Mom, can I have some of your water?"

By now the temperature of the water was so hot, she didn't even want it and was tired of carrying the two-liter bottle. However, she could not resist a motherly "I told you so."

The Princess could not believe the misery of the ordeal. Somehow she survived. Finally, she was at the bottom of Cardiac Hill. Her legs provided all the support of a bowl of Jell-O. Gladly, she sunk into her seat on the air-conditioned motor coach.

On the way to Ayres Rock, they stopped for lunch. The guide pulled two big coolers from the bus and set them in a picnic area. He announced, "Okay you have one hour to eat, clean up and get everything packed back on the bus." With that he left to mingle with other tour guides he knew. What kind of tour was this? They had to fix their own lunch!

The Princess was exhausted; she did not have the energy to expend preparing food. She would just sit in the grass with a Diet Coke and smoke. The Little Prince fixed them a sandwich, ham and cheese with mustard. This was no ordinary ham and cheese sandwich. This was no ordinary mustard. This was *fire* mustard. They had to get napkins and wipe away as much of the offending condiment as possible, through watery eyes and running noses.

Arriving at the permanent campsite, they got the next surprise. No bunk beds, just sleeping bags! And in a tent with poisonous snakes and spiders crawling everywhere! *Get me back to the Peace Corps!*

They made it back to Sydney for the last night together. The Little Prince checked his e-mail. He had been accepted to the Teach For America program. Upon graduation from Emory University in May, he would complete a training program and was assigned the Navajo Indian Reservation in New Mexico. He would be a third grade teacher during his two-year assignment. The Princess was very proud.

After a sad farewell in Sydney, the Princess flew to Auckland where she had a six-hour layover waiting for the Tongan airport to open Monday morning. She touched down in Tonga at 3:00 a.m. The Duchess had left the porch light on at the Princess's and placed a cup of wildflowers on her table. How thoughtful. The

Princess climbed in bed just in time for the first "erk, erk, erk, eeeerrrrkkkk" of the roosters.

TWO THOUSAND AND TWO

Upon the Princess's return, she was notified that the IA and the Commoner had both early terminated. She was not surprised by either one—the medical condition of the young girl was not good and she knew the IA was unhappy. The Canteen was not finished. It was under roof; just the inside still needed work. This would have to wait until school resumed.

Right outside her front door, the Princess had a tamarind tree. This held much fascination for the children of the neighborhood. They loved to climb way up into the branches for the pods, which contained seeds in a juicy acid pulp. They were very polite about this, always calling out to her from across the fence asking permission to ascend the trunk. Two little sisters were the most frequent visitors.

One Saturday while the Princess was baking cookies for the next afternoon's get together, she heard the girls calling her. Stepping onto the porch, she granted access to the tree along with a warm cookie for each. By the time she had returned to receive the next batch from the oven, she was again being summoned. Opening her screen door, she could scarcely believe her eyes. In the last five minutes about twenty-five small children had appeared! Each one wanted to taste the treat she had given the sisters. It's a good thing that when the Princess makes cookies, she really makes cookies.

Then, the Princess made the biggest mistake of her entire two years. It was a colossal blunder, a massive oversight, an incredible lapse of judgment. Having left her garden gloves outside on a wooden bench, she retrieved them and put first the left one on and then the right. Instantly, she realized the depth of her error.

Ripping off the offending right glove, out tumbled a six-inch *molokow*!!! The initial puncture, as the fangs pierced her finger, was like the stab of an ice pick being inserted with great force! Then, as the poison spread throughout the appendage, the searing heat of a vat of boiling oil could not have been greater! She screamed. She wept! She danced a jig! She invented new nasty words!

Within an hour her hand was so swollen, a new dread crept into the pit of her stomach!

The skin could not possibly stretch any further. There was a limit. What if it exploded and she was left, literally, with skin and bones! There is no comparison for the pain a molokow can inflict—not a bee sting, not a root canal; even childbirth was preferable.

She knew from M Squared that there is no cure but the passage of time. Ice was the only thing that would provide even slight relief. One-handed, she cracked the plastic trays into a bowl. She slept with a Ziploc bag of ice cubes in her bed that night. The swelling did not go down for two days. It was two weeks before she had full use of her hand again. How did her neighbor M Squared survive this on four separate occasions?

One Friday when the Princess arrived at the school there was much excitement. The staff had declared this would be Decoration Day. Each teacher let the students decorate their classrooms any way they chose. They didn't have much available to them: construction paper, crayons, Scotch tape, glue sticks and, of course, whatever Mother Nature provided around the campus.

Sita and the Princess proceeded from room to room. The classrooms were unadorned wooden structures with cement floors, a blackboard, blank walls, wooden desks and chairs. All the students were happily working on their contributions. They had created colored drawings and paper chains with crayons and construction paper. They were busy hanging their artwork all over the room. Some had done a more traditional Tongan decoration with palm fronds and flowers.

Every place they exited they were called into another. Ha'u! Ha'u! The Princess was amazed that such a simple idea as Decoration Day caused so much pleasure, gaiety and elation.

One of the teachers came up and threaded her arm through the Princess's. "You must come and see what my class has done."

When they entered the room, the noise ceased and the children all looked at the Princess expectantly. They were grinning from ear to ear. At first, she didn't see anything. The walls were still blank and there were no flowers. Glancing around she noticed everyone was looking up. So she too turned her gaze upward. Balloons were hanging from the ceiling. The students and teacher were waiting for a response. The Princess didn't know what to make of the balloons, they were different colors and they were inflated to different sizes. Then it hit her! "Oh my God!" she shouted, "it's the solar system!"

Cheers emitted from all. The Princess walked to the center of the room and pointed to a large yellow balloon. "That is the Sun. What planet is that?" The children identified each one in turn, in unison.

The Princess asked, who are the judges? The response was that there were no judges, that this was just for fun. Since this class was the only one that did something educational, she felt they deserved a prize. She gave Sita twenty pa'anga for this group to spend at the Canteen.

The Vaololoa Canteen was finally finished. The Princess used the same vendors she had delivering to Fasi, doubling the size of the orders. She had just enough left after construction to cover her opening inventory.

One more thing was needed before she could leave the Fasi campus: she needed someone to replace her there. Sita could not do all the bookkeeping and cook, sell, and clean alone. Her first employee had come from working in the library. There were no more surplus people. Sita suggested she knew a young girl who would be interested in the position.

"Great, have her come and talk to me."

The next day, Malama arrived. She was fresh from high school, having just graduated last year. This would be her first job. She was extremely shy. The Princess realized it was difficult for her to speak up. So the Princess decided to describe exactly what she expected and see if it was agreeable. It was not until she had spent twenty minutes explaining the requirements for the position that she began to suspect what Sita confirmed: Malama spoke almost *no* English. The Princess enlisted Sita to translate every word she uttered. Malama really wanted the job. Leaving Sita in charge, the Princess was free to open Vaololoa.

Vaololoa was a larger campus. There were more teachers and the students were much younger. Any staff member that had children under school age brought them to the school. It was more common than not to see a teacher writing at the chalkboard with a sleeping infant in the other arm. Strollers of sleeping toddlers were parked under shady trees. An older boy would sweep up a tiny fallen one, dry his tears and send him on his way again. There was an atmosphere more of a very extended family than of an institution.

Mapele had supplied her with a former student as the Vaololoa Canteen manager. Fifita was experienced, as she had worked in a food shop before. With the forty pa'anga a week the Princess was paying her, Fifita felt like a millionaire.

The Princess's father had designed and produced a bronze plaque commemorating every person whose donation had made the Canteen possible. It arrived the day before they opened. It was absolutely beautiful. The Tongans were quite impressed with it, never having seen many signs like it. They created a cement stand, angled at the top, in a place of honor in front of the Canteen.

At Fasi the students could swing by the Canteen between each class. At Vaololoa they were only permitted to make purchases before or after school and during lunchtime.

The first day they only sold eight pa'anga before first period. That was not good. The Princess started to get worried. Had she miscalculated the opportunities of this campus? Then at noon, an old-fashioned, handheld school bell was rung. *Lunchtime!*

Instantly, children exploded from classrooms all over the campus. All six hundred of them headed for the Canteen at the same time. The Princess and Fifita had only enough time to exchange a worried glance before they were mobbed. These kids ranged from six years up to about twelve. Kids are kids, whatever country they are in, whatever language they speak. They were pushing and shoving, all wanting to be first. The two clerks couldn't sell their wares fast enough. It was so exciting for that one hour during lunch. When the bell rang again signaling the end of the break, the children vanished.

Wow, they had some repair work to do. In their haste during the mad rush, they had tossed bags of goodies, snacks and coins around. Then they counted the money—in that one hour they had sold 190 pa'anga. Yee-haw, what a great start!

Exiting the marketi one afternoon, the Princess was on her way to the taxi stand. She could see about a dozen nice, clean taxis sitting there, waiting for a fare. Oh, no! There he was, John in that dilapidated car! She had been spotted. He was waving out of the window and calling her name. Oh, well, what is a Princess to do? She smiled as he assisted her with the broken door.

When they arrived at her home, as always, she slipped him a little extra money, hoping he would get the hint and start a fund for a new vehicle. No, no, he insisted, he could no longer let her overpay him. He had picked up a teacher from Tupou High the day before. She had told him the Princess was "an angel sent from God—what she did for the school!"

Oh, my! The Princess nearly burst into tears. That had to be the sweetest thing anyone had ever said to her.

That night, sharing dinner with her neighbors, she repeated what the taxi driver had said. They were not impressed and apparently, being an angel sent from God did not excuse you from washing the dishes.

Rumor had it that the Japanese government had given a vast amount of money to Tonga to replace the water system on the island. That sounded good, a free new water system and jobs for the Tongans to do the work. The bad part was that the Tongans had no training or experience with that sort of thing. They were not having great success with the newly laid pipes' performance.

Eventually, the installation of the new water works made its way out to the main road by Palangeville. From that day, everyone in her village had no water. With no tap water, they could not wash the dishes; they could not flush the toilet; they could not use the washing machine. If you didn't have a solar shower, which most did not, you could not take even a cold shower.

Though they still had the Cima tanks, everyone was now using that water for other uses besides drinking. They had to carry the water inside for everything. Five buckets of water had to be hauled from the Cima tank to the washing machine, then this process repeated for the rinse cycle. Besides being a burden, the water was running out.

This would never do. They notified the water board they had no water! The water board sent a Japanese guy and two Tongans to investigate. These three walked around the yard a few times with a map, then left. Still, they were without water. Again, they complained to the water board. This continued for two long weeks. Okay, that's it! The volunteers complained en masse to their employer.

The principal came out with the water board. They arrived at 2:00 p.m.; Feleti stood over them and would not let them knock off for the day at 5:00. He insisted they continue to dig until they could find the problem. At 9:00 that evening, Feleti knocked on the door of each person in Palangeville to verify they at last had water again.

The volunteers also heard that the Japanese government wanted to build Tonga a state-of-the-art hospital, something sorely needed. There was a catch. In exchange for this magnanimous gesture, they wanted whaling rights in the Tongan waters. The Tongans had no problem with that, since they were not very far thinking in the ways of ecology or environmental issues. However, every other country that funds a variety of projects in Tonga, such as Australia, New Zealand and America, did have a very large problem with that. The new hospital was out. The Princess never really knew how many or how much of these stories that she heard were actually true.

CLOSE OF SERVICE

Each Peace Corps group is together at the beginning and the end of their time of service. Each group, which can be anywhere from thirty to one hundred people, meets at the staging process. They are trained together, sworn in together and have the close of service together. Group 59 had only four volunteers left: the Duke, the Duchess, the Quiet One and the Princess. The two youngest members were no longer with them. So much for the Regional Director's prediction that the "older" volunteers had "little or no chance of completing their service."

The close of service was an all-day affair. Besides the remaining four volunteers, two of the trainers and the ACD and CD participated. After a large breakfast, they all adjourned to a meeting room. The APCD started off with several "get to know you" exercises, reliving when they had met each other for the first time. This was a lot of fun; in the last twenty-two months that the foursome had spent together, it would be difficult to know anyone better than they did. The APCD moved forward with a discussion of their feelings and expectations as they prepared to leave. They were advised to prepare for "reverse culture shock" when they returned to the United States.

The country director gave a speech: he hoped this group would feel as proud of themselves as he was of them. "It is impossible to know if a volunteer's contribution will leave a lasting effect," he told them. "Upon departure after two short years, you will probably never know if systems you put in place would continue without your driving force, if a person you trained or educated would incorporate the knowledge you gave them into their daily lives."

At the time of this group's service, Peace Corps accepted approximately one in five applications. Approximately thirty-five percent of those accepted dropped out worldwide. Group 59's two years were coming to a close. They had been steadfast. They were resolute. They had persevered.

Each person received a Completion of Service plaque, made by Tongans from the traditional tapa fabric.

After the ceremony, there was a large amount of administrative paperwork required. A Description of Service had to be completed and signed by the country director.

Then they went off to the bar, which they discovered had less than half a box of white wine left. The Quiet One switched to beer. He suggested to the Princess that they purchase the balance of the package, as this was the only alcoholic beverage she liked. The Princess responded, "Hmm, wouldn't that be rather selfish?" He laughed out loud, "To quote one of my best friends, what's your point?"

Ah, what had our Princess learned? She arrived in Tonga a selfish, spoiled brat. She was trained since birth that she was entitled to almost anything she desired. She had discovered that she is "entitled" to absolutely nothing.

Everything that is worth having cannot be given, it must be achieved on her own. The respect of her Tongan and volunteer coworkers—that had to be earned. Appreciating the beauty of another culture quite different from her own had to be learned. She knew she did not have to live in America to be an American. And, most of all, she learned it is never too late to become a better person.

After the cocktails they were treated to a buffet dinner served oceanfront. They stayed until midnight.

Days later the Duke and the Duchess prepared to depart. The Princess knew she would miss them. The Duke with his level head, intelligence, sense of humor and calm in the face of a crisis. Oh, how could she say goodbye to the Duchess? Her infectious laughter, her crazy ideas, and her screwball comedy, this would be like separating Lucy and Ethel!

Early morning they bid adieu. As the car pulled away the Princess wondered, to have known or not to have known. Is it better to suffer the slings and arrows of a painful parting, or never to have met someone?

The past two years flashed before her eyes. She had visions of training, home stay, swearing in, the roosters, flying pigs and wild dogs. Without the Duke and the

Duchess, how would she ever have survived? Yes, she decided it is better to have known.

Another new group arrived. The Quiet One would not be leaving; at the last minute he extended his service in Tonga for another year. He would be part of the training team for Group 63.

The Princess attended the official kava ceremony for these new recruits. Sitting on a straw mat surrounded by Tongan girls from the office, she could hardly believe it had been two years since she was the one being honored, with her legs curled off to her side growing numb, and apprehensive of tasting the kava.

Her job at Tupou High was finished. The two Canteens were functioning without her. The administrative office was computerized and running smoothly. She had nothing left to do but look over the trained Tongans' shoulders. It was time to go.

Having drinks with her APCD, she confessed, she was no longer needed here, but she could not bear to return to a boring, mundane life in America. Her APCD had a suggestion.

"Reenroll. Go to another Peace Corps assignment. Take on a new challenge in another country."

She was lifted out of her depression. This was just the thing for our Princess. Something else to strive for, another quest, a new adventure! After all, this Princess still loved to travel and she liked living abroad. Also, she now knew exactly just how "tough" it could get. She would be a better volunteer next time.

So the next day the Princess contacted Washington, D.C. She filed all the reenrollment paperwork, completed her new essays and obtained references from her CD, APCD and other volunteers. Before leaving Tonga she received an e-mail from Washington. She was transferred into another assignment!

So, as the Princess buckled her seat belt, she taxied down the only runway in Nuku'alofa, Tonga for the last time. She was once again winging her way toward her destiny. She thought to herself,

LET THE ADVENTURE BEGIN!

FROM THE DUKE & THE DUCHESS, RENWICK NELSON & BRENDA SUE DREW

What does it take to have a successful Peace Corps experience? That is an interesting question that may have many answers, but I believe a successful Peace Corps volunteer will have many of the qualities of any other successful person. The volunteer should be flexible, adaptable, intelligent, joyful, and empathetic; she should be happy with small achievements, believe that the American way is not the only way and have a sense of humor. If I may, I would like to explain what is meant by each of the terms I have used.

Flexibility is the ability to change your plans. In the Peace Corps, many projects seem well planned at first glance but they aren't. The volunteer must be able to change or reinvent projects so she has a chance to be successful with the people and resources she has available.

Adaptability is the ability to not only survive but also thrive on dealing with the unexpected and with new experiences. You may be required to live with others of different cultures with habits you may find distasteful, deal with situations you have never experienced, etc. An example may help. How do you get rid of an unwanted pig (not the human variety) that believes your home is his home?

Intelligence does not refer to your IQ as much as your ability to think through situations to enable you to solve problems you will face almost daily. This will require analysis and original thinking or, as many modern business people say, "thinking outside of the box."

A joyful person is one who can find happiness and satisfaction in the small things in life, such as the smile of a child, the look on a student's face when she first understands something you are teaching or the beauty of a simple life.

Empathy is the ability to walk in someone else's shoes and truly feel and understand what they are feeling. With this quality, you may better understand why the local people won't do things the way you want them done.

A Peace Corps volunteer must be happy, and this requires that she be happy with small achievements like getting a student to read his homework or buying a fresh piece of fruit. Most of us never see huge steps or advancements. These things take much more time than two years. If you are happy and sincerely praise the small achievements of others, you are much more effective and your presence will be more meaningful for those around you. If you can't be happy, *leave*. You are doing no good for yourself or those you come in contact with.

You must recognize that the American way, whatever you think it means, is but one way of living or doing and not always the best way. You are not there to help others experience our ways and cultures, but for you to experience their ways and cultures and help everyone choose what is best for them. Don't be the ugly American who wears blinders and is unable to see and experience all the wonders of a new and exciting culture.

Last but not least, and maybe even most, you must have a sense of humor about yourself and your life as a volunteer. This doesn't mean you won't complain or have doubts, but it simply means that you must be able to laugh at yourself and the situations you find yourself in. Remember that this is a joyful and eye-opening experience that requires that you laugh.

This book is about a spoiled older American rich kid who was able to keep her sense of humor and is now sharing it with you. By the way, she was successful because of her attributes and her ability to recognize her own small achievements. Only time will tell if her small achievements will blossom into big achievements that will have a lasting effect on those she worked and lived with.

The Duke and Duchess

978-0-595-41869-5
0-595-41869-4

Printed in the United States
85877LV00004B/343-345/A